Managers
As
Facilitators

Managers *As* Facilitators

A Practical Guide to

Getting Work Done in a

Changing Workplace

Richard G. Weaver & John D. Farrell

Berrett-Koehler Publishers, Inc.
San Francisco

Berrett-Koehler Publishers, Inc.
450 Sansome Street, Suite 1200
San Francisco, CA 94111-3320
Tel: (415) 288-0260   Fax: (415) 362-2512   www.bkpub.com

Ordering Information
Individual sales. Berrett-Koehler publications are available through most bookstores. They can also be ordered direct from Berrett-Koehler at the address above.

Quantity sales. Special discounts are available on quantity purchases by corporations, associations, and others. For details, contact the "Special Sales Department" at the Berrett-Koehler address above.

Orders for college textbook/course adoption use. Please contact Berrett-Koehler Publishers at the address above.

Orders by U.S. trade bookstores and wholesalers. Please contact Publishers Group West, 1700 Fourth Street, Berkeley, CA 94710. Tel: (510) 528-1444. Fax: (510) 528-9555.

Printed in the United States of America
Printed on acid-free and recycled paper that is composed of 50% recovered fiber, including 10% post consumer waste.

Library of Congress Cataloging-in-Publication Data
Weaver, Richard G., 1947-
    Managers as facilitators : a practical guide to getting work done in a changing workplace / Richard G. Weaver & John D. Farrell. — 1st ed.
      p.   cm.
    Includes bibliographical references and index.
    ISBN 1-57675-016-7 (hardcover: alk. paper)
    ISBN 1-57675-054-X (paperback:alk paper)
      1. Teams in the workplace. 2. Decision-making, Group. 3. Supervision of employees. I. Farrell, John D., 1960-   . II. Title
HD66.W4   1997
658.4'036—dc21   97-2306
                                            CIP

First Hardcover Printing: May 1997
First Paperback Printing: December 1998

03 02 01 00 99 98   10 9 8 7 6 5 4 3 2 1

Production supervisor: Carol Dondrea   Cover photo: PhotoDisc
Interior design: Suzanne Montazer   Composition: Christi Payne Fryday
Cover design: Karen Marquardt   Indexing: John Dibs

This paperback contains the complete text of of the original hardcover edition

To Patti, my partner, my friend, and my love
R.G.W.

To my wife, Laurie, and the friendship and love we share
J.D.F.

Contents

P A R T   I I
New Insights into Facilitation   145

Tables and Figures

Tables

Figures

Preface

*T*he workplace is changing. For managers in almost every organization these changes are sometimes exciting, sometimes painful. Managers are expected to do new things in new ways with fewer people and fewer dollars. The old ways of managing—specifying work and closely supervising its completion—just do not work as well now. Most managers have not only more people reporting directly to them than ever before, but also more demands on their time. It is simply not practical for managers to tell people exactly how they must complete their tasks. There is simply not enough time.

The amount of work demanded is more than individuals can produce working alone. This need to get more people working better with others has led to the creation of a great number of teams. Some teams have been quite effective, whereas others have not. In fact, the experience in many cases has been so bad that many people react negatively to the word *team* itself. For that reason, we generally avoid that term in this book and use *group* instead.

This is not another book on groups. It is a book about helping individuals in organizations work more effectively together. It is a practical guide to getting work done in this changing workplace.

Helping groups complete their work and improve the ways they work together is a new role for many managers. We call this role **facilitator.** It is quite different from the traditional manager role, which "plans, directs, and controls." It is also different from the traditional leader role, which "sets vision, tone, and direction." Managers know they are being asked to do things differently. But most have never been trained in helping groups get their work done. Some have done well because of their experience and natural talents; others have struggled.

Facilitating is much more than running smooth meetings. *Effective facilitation is about helping people get their work done*, whether it is done in groups, with a few people, or alone. *It is also about helping people work together more effectively.* As expected, this work takes place in group meetings, but it also takes place in other settings, including informal gatherings and one-on-one meetings. Facilitators help groups be clear about the work to be done, who will do it, and how it will be completed.

Can groups really work? If they can, what needs to happen to help them and their organizations succeed? We have worked with a number of organizations around the world to help them answer these questions. We have found three critical elements that impact the success of groups:

1. The people in organizations who establish groups—often senior executives—must operate differently than in the past. They need to create opportunities for the groups to succeed by paying more than lip service to appropriate collaborative efforts. They must be clear what is expected from each group, hold the groups accountable, and recognize group achievements.

2. Individuals need the skills and knowledge that will help them join groups quickly, contribute productively, and then leave smoothly. They have to learn how to work more collaboratively.

3. People who act in the facilitator role have a very different function from those in the traditional manager or leader roles. Facilitators have to understand how individuals and groups operate and know practical skills to help them get their work done. This book focuses on this third critical element.

We have found that effective facilitation has a much bigger impact on the success of groups than traditional "team-building" activities. This is especially true when the person in the facilitator role also has a leader or manager role. Why? Because the manager as facilitator bridges the gap between group members and executives. If a group's assignment is unclear, a manager who understands and uses the facilitator role can help the group get the answers it needs. If a group gets stuck, an effective facilitator can help the group get going again.

Many individuals struggle because they try to facilitate without a clear sense of how facilitating differs from leading and managing. They become frustrated and their groups disillusioned. They associate facilitation with "touchy-feely" activities and organization-wide "feel-good" sessions that are a waste of time and money. They have not experienced the practical, productive side of facilitation.

Others assume that facilitation is simply having a sufficiently large stock of tools that can be selected when a group becomes bogged down. Most facilitator training programs and books on facilitator training we have seen are limited to describing such tools and how to use them. This approach does not recognize the important interpersonal dynamics that are part of every group's work.

In organizations around the world, effective facilitation helps groups complete real work by creating a balance. It does not focus on encouraging group members to "bare their soul" or limit itself to using tools. Effective facilitation reflects a practical set of skills and knowledge that helps people work together better to complete real work.

Why we feel passionate about facilitation

We have each had a wide variety of facilitation experiences, and we have seen many good results from effective facilitation. We have discovered facilitation processes that work across diverse cultural situations. We know what works and what does not work. We have facilitated groups throughout the United States and also in Europe, Asia, Africa, and South America. Helping groups achieve a whole new level of success by using facilitation has been a powerful experience for us.

Watching groups flounder, disintegrate, and even sabotage the work of others has also had a powerful impact on us. In these settings, where we were not facilitating, we saw productive opportunities being lost and people being hurt. They were pulling back, no longer offering their full capability to the organization or to each other. Real success was becoming harder to achieve. In some of these situations, the people responsible were determined to do it their own way, oblivious to how badly it was going. In other situations, the people responsible were frustrated with the outcomes and wanted to do it very differently—but they did not know how.

We found that as we offered training courses in effective facilitation, people with many different roles in organizations attended. They told us that what they learned helped them and their organizations. They were excited as they experienced new successes. These results have greatly boosted our commitment to share our approach to facilitation.

Developing this book

Over the past four years, we developed and refined a series of training workshops to help individuals learn this new role. We developed a model for describing how effective facilitation works. We incorporated concepts we learned from others. Then we added boundary management and change management to these concepts.

As we worked with more and more people, the material grew in two important ways: It got both theoretically deeper *and* more practical. Both we and our clients kept asking, "How can I actually use this?" Everyone got excited about how useful the information proved to be. Clients told us that our concepts of facilitation were making a big difference for them.

We knew there was a book to be written—a book that could be helpful to the many individuals who are adding the facilitation role to their jobs. As professional consultants, trainers, and facilitators, it is important to us that this book be both practical and useful to you.

Who is this book for?

This book is primarily for individuals who need to be facilitators in addition to their other roles. We expect the people who have position titles such as supervisor, manager, or director to find this book most useful. They are on the front line of the effort to get people to work together more productively. For them, we have deliberately filled the book with practical ways of solving problems.

We also expect professional consultants and facilitators to find this book helpful. The many new models presented here will be useful in their work.

This book is for people who know that facilitation can make a difference. It is for people who want to improve their skills and help their organizations, whether they are working in companies driven by the "bottom line" or in public and private not-for-profit organizations.

How to use this book

We know that few people have the time to read a book from cover to cover unless it is a novel read on vacation. Work-related books are idea sources, thinking stimulators, and references. Although we invite you to read this book from beginning to end, that approach is not necessary to find practical ideas and approaches that will help you be a better facilitator.

The Introduction chapter explores the realities of this new facilitator role and how it must often be balanced with the roles of manager and leader. Establishing and maintaining this balance is demanding. However, the rewards for doing the job well are very exciting.

Chapters 1 through 8 present the elements of our Facilitation Model. The central element of the model is **Task** (Chapter 1). A group begins by considering the tasks assigned to it, and relates all subsequent activities to accomplishing those tasks. Charge and Charter (Chapter 2) presents ways to clarify the tasks. Facilitators must have a clear sense of **Self** (Chapters 3 and 4). This means they know themselves well and know how they impact others. They need to appreciate the differences in others. The third element of the model is **Group**. Facilitators must be aware of group dynamics—of how group members interact (Chapter 5). They must know what is normal for groups, especially if the behaviors are considered problems. Responding productively to conflict (Chapter 6) is a critical dynamic in successful groups. **Process** is the final element (Chapter 7) of our Facilitation Model. Process describes how groups get work done and includes both procedures and a tool box for facilitators. Helping groups listen more effectively (Chapter 8) greatly contributes to productivity. Each element in the model interacts with and impacts the others. Understanding how to use this model leads to constructive action that will help groups complete their work.

Chapters 9 through 11 are designed to give facilitators additional skills and assistance. Defining facilitation as boundary management is a radical way to describe facilitation in work settings (Chapter 9). Responding to or creating change is a constant part of the life of every individual and group. Chapter 10 provides new ways of looking both at change processes and the impact of change on individuals, groups, and organizations. Special attention is given to dealing with "resistors." The final chapter of the book (Chapter 11) is a reference section that identifies 15 of the most challenging facilitation problems and gives recommendations for action. Readers are also directed to other sections of the book for more information on each problem.

The book is filled with examples of people working to fulfill this new facilitator role. Taken one at a time, the examples may seem small or even insignificant. And, it is true, no single facilitator action is likely to have a huge impact on the success of an entire organization. However, we have observed that change rarely comes from a single—no matter how heroic—act. Rather, it is the sum total of these day-to-day actions that have made a big difference in the productivity and satisfaction of facilitators and those with whom they work.

You can make a difference as an effective facilitator

In spite of the painful experiences some individuals and organizations have had with groups and teams, we believe these work structures are here to stay. Effective facilitation is the key to helping groups break through to new levels of productivity. It is not magic, however— although many people have told us that it seems like that as they look in from the outside on a highly skilled facilitator. There are practical things people can do to learn this role.

We know that anyone can learn to be an excellent facilitator. We know that novices can become good facilitators and that good facilitators can become even better. Effective facilitation helps groups learn how to operate differently, build on each other's talents, and achieve the seemingly impossible. As an effective facilitator, you can make a huge difference. We invite you to use this book to help you make that difference.

Acknowledgments

To write about something that we feel passionate about is a gift we treasure. And we feel passionate about facilitation! However, we know that facilitation does not occur in isolation, and a book on facilitation has to be the product of a collaboration that goes far beyond two authors.

We acknowledge David Anderson, Eileen Hogan, and Kathleen Razi, who shared in that bright moment when we created the first Facilitation Model. We are also indebted to David Anderson, Peggy Christensen, Jon Kemske, Shelly Regan, Jolanta Sears, and Michael Ryan for pouring over early drafts and giving us invaluable feedback. You helped us focus on being practical. We have seen the improvements that have come from the reviews of Berrett-Koehler's Steven Piersanti, Stan Bass, Andrea Markowitz, Jennifer Myers, Sara Jane Hope, and Robert Zane. Carol Dondrea's copyediting has been exceptional. You have guided this book into what it is today.

Dick wishes to give special acknowledgment to the support and encouragement of his family: Robert and Mary Weaver, Barbara Weaver, Marti Scrivens, and John Weaver. You have always believed in my ability to create and to be of service; it has made a difference. Faith Ralston, William Randall Beard, and Elleva Joy McDonald, writers and facilitators in your own right, have been all that I could ask for from friends. And Patti Christensen, who has had faith and confidence that I was a writer and a willingness to read just one more draft chapter, thank you.

John wishes to give special acknowledgment to the support and encouragement of his family and children: Robert and Helen Farrell, Bill and Ginger Brashear, Brad Brashear, Robin Hampton, Anne Strid, Brian Kranz, Julia Farrell, and Joseph Farrell. Your support and belief in my ability has given me strength and confidence. David Anderson, an outstanding manager and facilitator, has contributed in so many ways. And Laurie, who has given so much to our home and family and helped me be a better husband, father, and partner, thank you.

Finally, we wish to acknowledge the remarkable relationship that continues to grow between us as coauthors, professional colleagues, and, most of all, friends.

Richard Weaver and John Farrell
March 1997

INTRODUCTION

Facilitator: The Important New Role for Managers

In this Introduction you will learn:

- Why facilitator is an important new role for managers
- The differences among the roles of leader, manager, and facilitator
- A Facilitation Model that describes the role
- The behaviors, beliefs, and values of effective facilitators

*F*acilitator is the most important role to emerge in the modern workplace. The workplace is changing as never before, and mastering the role of facilitator has helped leaders and managers respond successfully to these changes. Effective facilitators are able to help individuals, groups, and entire organizations get their work done in the face of such changes. Skilled facilitators help groups improve the quality and quantity of their work by getting members to work together more effectively.

Today's workplace is a place of change. Unprecedented global competition and the rapid deployment of new technology are forcing organizations to reconfigure themselves in order to remain vibrant and competitive. Restructuring is one way in which organizations have been meeting these challenges. Although restructuring itself is not a new phenomenon, the extent and frequency with which it has been happening *is* new. Nearly everyone who works—whether in the public or private sector—has been touched by restructuring or one of its variations: reengineering, downsizing, right-sizing, and so on.

1

How has the modern workplace been affected by restructuring? The pace of work is faster and more furious. Managers have to deal with a staggering amount of information. They have far more responsibilities and far fewer resources to get the job done. Yet, managers who understand the art and science of facilitation are doing more than surviving in this environment—they are thriving. They use their facilitation skills to help their groups get their work done in new and innovative ways. Managers who fail to learn facilitation skills are getting buried. Their traditional "direct and control" approach to managing just does not work when there is so much to do and so little time to do it.

More and more companies are marketing their products and services in the global marketplace. Managers thus have more customers to satisfy, and the increasing demands of those customers are changing the way companies operate. Organizations that fail to meet the rising expectations of their customers are soon replaced by those that can. Organizations with managers who are skilled facilitators are faring well in the global marketplace. They are better able to listen to customers—whether those customers are in Montana or Malaysia.

Technology is rapidly changing the way people work together. Today, it is common for work groups to be geographically dispersed. Meetings frequently take place over the phone, and sales transactions are made via e-mail. Managers who are skilled facilitators are able to help groups use technology to be more productive and stay connected with one another.

Managers who are skilled facilitators use their knowledge of organizational change processes to help others deal with the emotional side of change, enabling people to focus on their work. These skilled facilitators help groups clarify their goals. It is extremely valuable to people who feel as if the very ground is shifting beneath them to have facilitators help them focus on a few well-defined goals. Managers who are skilled facilitators provide a calming influence *and* practical methods to deal with the aftermath of restructuring.

What specifically are these managers doing differently? How does being an effective facilitator help these managers deal with their fast-paced world? How is the role of facilitator different from the roles of leader and manager? How can understanding the differences among the three roles help people be more productive? What results are being delivered by managers who are good facilitators? We begin to answer these questions by first looking at the definition of facilitation itself.

Facilitation

What is facilitation? **Facilitation is a process through which a person helps others complete their work and improve the way they work together.** Facilitators help others get their work done. They provide methods that support both accomplishing tasks *and* helping individuals work together. Although any given situation may emphasize one aspect more heavily than the other, facilitators help people pay attention to both things in the long run. Facilitators help people make the connection between the quality of their work and the way they treat each other as they work together.

Facilitator as a distinct role from leader and manager

Facilitator is a distinct role and not just a subset of management skills. Recognizing this distinction is critical to using facilitation well. People do things in the facilitator role that are sometimes in direct conflict with what they would do in either the traditional "direct and control" manager role or the "big picture" leader role. If individuals fail to be clear about the role they are using in a particular situation, others will be confused.

Distinguishing the roles is important for another reason. All three roles are essential for organizations who hope to succeed. Organizations need people in the leader role to take the long-term view, set the tone, and point in the right direction. They need people in the manager role to pay attention to the here and now, plan well, and set the pace. And they need people in the facilitator role to help the work get done. More and more organizations need their people to master all three roles.

Consider the challenge that faced a manager following a major restructuring at an international technology firm. Before the restructuring, she managed 12 salespeople in a territory covering seven states. After restructuring, she was assigned a new job: managing a new cross-functional group with people from sales, marketing, and technical service.

"My company has always managed performance based on individual contributions. Now I am required to manage my people's performance based on a combination of organization, group, and individual goals. This is a major change. I've already heard from one group member that he is worried about having to carry the load for those who slack off." She knew that she faced an uphill battle getting her new group excited about its goals because members were still trying to cope with the sweeping changes of the restructuring, as she was herself.

During the group's first meeting, members spent a lot of time talking about how the restructuring had affected them. Some people were sad and others were angry. The manager encouraged them to vent their feelings for a while, participating herself in the discussion. Later in the meeting, she told them about the assignment her new boss had given them. She then initiated a discussion about how the group would go about completing the assignment, using the Charge and Charter methodology described in Chapter 2. The manager used the role of facilitator to help group members support one another during this difficult time *and* make progress on their assignment.

Her considerable management skills helped her, too. She was able to conceive of a plan necessary to complete the assignment. Instead of doing the project plans and budgets herself, however, she helped people in her new group develop and use these skills themselves. "The biggest challenge I had was to learn how to facilitate the work of others, and then trust that they were doing it right. As I got to be a better facilitator, the trust I showed my group got to be contagious. We learned to count on one another. We got a reputation for being easy to work with, so people outside of the group responded a little more quickly to our requests for help."

This manager's group was one of the few to make its revenue goal the first year after restructuring. "Two years ago the question I asked the most was, 'When will you have this done?' Now I ask, 'What are you trying to accomplish and how will that help the group fulfill its purpose?' I'm still concerned about deadlines. I just make sure we're working on the right things."

What are the practical things she did in her role as facilitator? This manager learned new tools and methods to help her group complete its work. Rather than trying to do all of the work herself, which was no longer possible, she *helped her group* do things such as:

- Clarify tasks
- Redefine the roles of its members
- Plan meetings
- Learn to work together better

- Plan projects
- Finish work (come to closure)
- Make decisions

- Map processes
- Resolve conflicts
- Make sense of piles of information

In addition, she used her leader and manager roles appropriately. How did she know to do this? To answer this question we must first explore the differences among the roles of leader, manager, and facilitator.

Comparing the three roles: Leader, manager, and facilitator

Table I-1 (page 6) provides a quick comparison of the three distinct roles of leader, manager, and facilitator. Most people who have a managerial title use all three roles to do their work. It is challenging to integrate the roles of leader, manager, and facilitator because the roles themselves sometimes conflict, both in subtle and profound ways.

Leaders are concerned with doing the right thing, managers are concerned with doing things right, and facilitators are concerned with helping people do things. The leader role sets tone and direction, the manager role sets the pace, and the facilitator role helps people make meaning of the tone and direction while helping them get their work done at the required pace. Individuals who are not being clear about the role they are using can confuse people, damage trust, and hurt productivity.

Moving between roles

How does a person actually move from role to role while working with a group? We recommend that people simply announce their intention of changing roles. Spending a few minutes discussing which is the best role for a particular situation helps the group understand what is going on. If the individual acting as the facilitator needs to make a suggestion from the role of leader or manager, he or she can just announce the shift in roles.

One group leader we worked with struggled so much with this transition that he made himself a hat with the title "FACILITATOR" in bold letters. If he felt the need to switch to his group leader role while facilitating a meeting, he would literally remove his hat. This helped

Table I-1 *Comparing the roles of leader, manager, and facilitator*

Leader	Manager	Facilitator
Concerned with doing the right thing	Concerned with doing things right	Concerned with helping people do things
Takes the long-term view	Takes the short-term view	Helps people find a view and articulate it
Concentrates on what and why	Concentrates on how	Helps people concentrate and be clear in the here and now
Thinks in terms of innovation, development, and the future	Thinks in terms of administration, maintenance, and the present	Helps people think, and helps them communicate their thoughts
Sets the vision: the tone and direction	Sets the plan: the pace	Helps people make meaning of tone and direction, and to function well at the required pace
Hopes others will respond and follow	Hopes others will complete their tasks	Hopes others will engage in the process
Appeals to hopes and dreams	Monitors boundaries and defines limits	Helps others make meaning of hopes and dreams; pushes appropriately on boundaries
Expects others to help realize a vision	Expects others to fulfill their mission or purpose	Helps others articulate a shared vision and common mission or purpose
Inspires innovation	Inspires stability	Helps people respond to things that are new and things that remain the same

both him and the group be clear about his role at any given moment. Group members could discern which hat he was wearing at any time and make observations about the consistency of his behavior within his role. With practice, the need for actually using the hat went away.

People should not bounce from role to role too often in a given situation, however. We have observed that managers who are inexperienced with the role of facilitator sometimes change roles too many times during a meeting, especially when they feel the group moving in a new or different direction. Transitioning too often can undermine trust within the group. As a practical guideline, for a given work session or meeting, one primary role should be used. Some groups use Table I-1 to help them decide which role will be most helpful for the task at hand.

Factors influencing the choice of role

What is the best role for a given situation? Managers must look at the *nature of the tasks* for which they are responsible. If the task is setting direction for a group—helping group members see the bigger picture—then the leader role is best. If the task is setting limits on the work, delegating, or defining deadlines, then the manager role should be the choice. If the task is more complex, requiring the assistance of a number of other people to complete it, then the facilitator role is best.

Another factor to consider when choosing the appropriate role is the *degree of support needed from others.* Support comes in many forms. The manager role carries with it authority that can automatically produce compliance with decisions. A supportive response to a decision by a manager might sound like this: "My boss decided that I should do this. I'm going to do what she asked." In many cases, the degree of support coming from such compliance is sufficient to complete a task. During a workday filled with tens of decisions, people often appreciate being told what to do.

If the degree of support for an initiative must spread widely across the organization, then the leader role is best. Remember from Table I-1 that the leader role is used to take the long-term view, set direction, and inspire innovation. The leader role is thus most useful for building broad support.

When a deeper level of support is needed, the facilitator role works best. A higher level of participation creates commitment—rather than compliance—to completing a task and reaching a desired outcome. People feel more responsibility for something they help create. Using the facilitator role is the most efficient, effective, and practical way to build strong support.

Another factor to consider when choosing the roles of leader, manager, or facilitator is the *stage of the group's development*. Less developed groups tend to need more direction from the leader role and control from the manager role. If group members are less experienced working in effective groups, they will be more productive if the individual in charge uses the manager role. More developed groups, which have the skills and experience to work with less direction, tend to respond well to a person using the facilitator role. Such groups have a track record of success and know what to do. With this more developed group, the facilitator can leave the technical content of the work to the group and concentrate on helping members work together more effectively.

A common problem for managers who are new to facilitation is the tendency to overuse the facilitator role. A manager with a consumer products company was told one day by a group member, "You know, we don't have to decide everything as a group. We're afraid you are going to set up a brainstorming meeting the next time one of us wants to buy a new pencil! It would be a relief if you would just make some of these decisions and delegate like you used to. You are a good manager. Keep using your skills."

The manager, who was still feeling uncomfortable with the role of facilitator, was encouraged by this nudge to go back to more familiar territory. For a while, he seldom used the role of facilitator and quickly abandoned it if he felt things were going in the wrong direction. But this behavior did not work either—as he heard from more than one group member. Exasperated, he later told a colleague, "I'm damned if I do and damned if I don't! What do these people want from me?"

Because his newly formed group was inexperienced in working as a group, the colleague suggested that he use the manager role more often than the facilitator role. Furthermore, the colleague counseled that once the manager chose to use the facilitator role, he should stick with it. "The next time you facilitate, stay in the role no matter what happens. Your group is not going to wreck the place. They might even do something great." This turned out to be helpful advice. He soon found the right balance for using the roles.

The manager role and leader role cannot be neglected. These roles are needed to varying extents, regardless of the nature of the task, the support needed from others, or the stage of group development. Acting in the leader role, an individual sets or clarifies the desired outcomes of the group. The person using the manager role is ultimately accountable for the completion of tasks. Managers are responsible for the outcomes and, therefore, responsible for the work necessary to accomplish them. Because they have a stake in the successful completion of tasks, those using the leader role and manager role are never neutral observers.

In contrast, the facilitator has to let the group be responsible for its tasks. Allowing this to happen is one of the most difficult things managers struggle with as they learn to facilitate. Once they assume the role of facilitator, they must help the group do its work, trusting and supporting the outcome the group creates. We have observed that, in times of stress or uncertainty, managers abandon the facilitator role too quickly. This problem usually results from failure of the manager role to clearly define the limits for the work. The manager attempting to facilitate can more easily stay in the role of facilitator if he or she has clearly defined those limits.

Knowing *when* to choose the role of facilitator is critical. Knowing *how* to do it well is what the rest of this book is all about.

The Facilitation Model

Our Facilitation Model provides the basis for successfully fulfilling the role of facilitator. It points out practical things to do every day to produce the results people want and need. Figure I-1 (on page 10) shows the model we created to illustrate the critical elements of facilitation and show how those elements are related.

Task is at the center of the model because helping people be clear about their task is the single most important thing a facilitator does. Every action facilitators take should help groups move closer to completing that task. Facilitators constantly ask themselves, "Is this action going to help the group complete its task?"

If you remember only one thing from this book, make sure it is this: *Facilitators should always help groups be clear about their tasks.*

Figure I-1 Facilitation Model

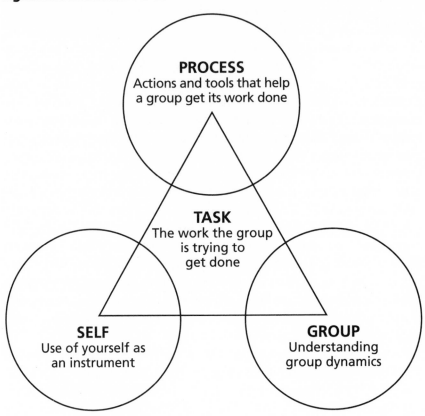

If you do that, you'll be fulfilling the role of facilitator better than most people who work full time as facilitators or consultants.

The most powerful and useful tool facilitators bring into a situation is themselves. For this reason, **Self** is one of the elements of the model. Facilitators must know themselves and how they impact their groups. They frequently ask themselves the question, "What do I think is going on here? How do I feel about what is happening at this moment?" They occasionally share the answer to this question with the group—if it will help members complete their task.

The Self element is also important in understanding how people are alike and how they are different. Although every individual is unique, certain general work style preferences that can be described and understood are common to almost everyone. Effective facilitators use this knowledge to help group members consider their similarities *and* differences as assets they can use to get their work done.

Group is another element of the Facilitation Model. Certain group dynamics are unique to the group in which they occur, but much of what happens in groups is predictable. Understanding these group dynamics is essential to facilitators in helping people get their work done more effectively. Facilitators ask themselves, "Have I seen this kind of behavior before, in this group or other groups?" As they gain more experience, facilitators learn to recognize typical dynamics. They help people become aware of how they are functioning and help them take steps to improve. Underlying all of this is a continuing focus on task. Such a focus creates more alignment within a group, making it easier for people to talk about emotions and be supportive of one another. The normal emotional energy available to people becomes a practical asset in helping get the work done.

Conflict is such an important aspect of the Group element of the Facilitation Model that we devote an entire chapter to it (see Chapter 6). Effective facilitators know how to help groups experience conflict as a productive, normal, and necessary occurrence and use it to their advantage.

The fourth and final element of the facilitation model is **Process**. Facilitators use their knowledge of Task, Self, and Group to decide which facilitation process to use with a group. Process is a set of actions or tools, an exercise, or an intervention that helps groups progress toward their goals. In Chapter 7, we review three fundamental facilitation processes: planning, solving problems, and finishing work.

The most important facilitation skill is *active listening*. In Chapter 8, we give you practical ways to improve your ability to listen to others. Listening well is essential if you are to choose the right facilitation tool at the right time. The best facilitators are active listeners.

The Facilitation Model takes a complex role and breaks it down into four simpler elements: Task, Self, Group, and Process. Although we devote two chapters to each element, you do not need to know each element in great detail in order to be an effective facilitator. As you dive into the book, you will be reminded of the relationship among the elements. More importantly, you will be given practical tips, advice, and actions you can take to fulfill this role.

Values, beliefs, and behaviors of effective facilitators

Effective facilitators share a common set of values, beliefs, and behaviors. The best facilitators we have trained, observed, and worked with have consistently demonstrated these values, beliefs, and behaviors.

We define **values** as "what people consider to be important." Effective facilitators value collaboration. They value people and honor differences among them. Facilitators value helping others build on good relationships to get their work done. Those who try to facilitate without these values are much more likely to create frustration for themselves and the people with whom they work.

We define **beliefs** as "what people think is true; what is their reality." An effective facilitator believes he or she is in a supporting role. *The facilitator's job is to help the group be the star.* The facilitator believes that people function best when they use their individual differences as assets rather than liabilities. The effective facilitator also believes that a group must be clear about its task in order to perform well.

We define **behaviors** as "what people do that we can observe." Values and beliefs drive specific behaviors. Above all, facilitators behave in a helping manner. They treat the group in a respectful, encouraging way. Facilitators constantly monitor what is going on, listening to and observing all of the signals. They avoid judging others. Facilitators are aware of their effect on others and use their presence consciously and appropriately. Facilitators know when to intervene more strongly and when to be silent. They think ahead before speaking or acting. They first ask themselves, "What impact will this action have on the group?"

At the beginning of this introduction, we asserted that facilitator is the most important role to emerge in the modern workplace. The rest of this book will help you learn how to fulfill this very challenging, rewarding, and practical role.

The Essential Elements of Facilitation

*T*he four essential elements of facilitation are presented in Part I. Our Facilitation Model shows how these four elements are related. The central element of facilitation is **Task.** Facilitators help people get their work done by assisting them to clarify their task (Chapter 1). A task might be as simple as completing one step of a project or as complex as defining the overall purpose of a work group. It is surprising how much people struggle with this—and how much productivity is lost because of the struggle. Applying Charge and Charter (Chapter 2) is a practical and effective approach for helping groups complete tasks.

The second essential element of facilitation is **Self.** Facilitators must understand themselves and recognize how they can intentionally use themselves to help groups become more productive (Chapter 3). A key part of better understanding themselves and their group members is recognizing and benefiting from differences (Chapter 4). Groups need these differences in order to be most successful.

Group is the third essential element of facilitation. Each group has unique characteristics and many common dynamics. Through their understanding of group dynamics, facilitators can help people develop into a cohesive, productive, healthy work group (Chapter 5). Conflict is one of the most common problems faced by groups. Effective facilitators know how to help groups use conflict to actually improve their productivity (Chapter 6).

The fourth essential element of facilitation is **Process.** Process is defined as "what a facilitator does to help a group get its work done." Facilitators use a variety of tools to accomplish this. Planning, solving problems, and finishing work are three fundamental processes facilitators use to help people complete their tasks (Chapter 7). The most critical skill for facilitators is to listen effectively (Chapter 8).

It is in learning more about each of these four essential elements and then synthesizing them that facilitators are able to help groups improve their productivity and work together more effectively. Understanding and using these four essential elements help facilitators move beyond the tentative, often awkward, beginning stages of facilitation. They then respond well, even in the most challenging situations, to help their groups successfully complete their work.

CHAPTER 1

Facilitators Focus on Task

In this chapter you will learn how to:

- Help a group be clear about its task
- Establish a contract between a facilitator and group

*W*e define Task as **the work a group needs to complete**. The facilitator's first job is to know what task people want and need to complete. Task exists on more than one level. The overall group assignment (for example, develop a new product) is one level of task. The action steps that a group completes every day (for example, an experiment testing a proposed product design) is another level of task. Facilitators help groups define and complete tasks on these various levels. Only by knowing the task can a facilitator choose the most helpful, practical actions.

As simple as this sounds, failing to be clear about the task is a common obstacle to groups getting their work done. Facilitators are in an excellent position to help groups quickly become clear about their work so they can do it well.

Consider the experience of a senior manager in a state government agency whose project assignment was to "develop a technology vision" for the organization. She was given a 90-day deadline to complete a document that would describe this vision. The vision was intended to guide the organization in making technology-related decisions. A number of managers from different departments were expected to assist her in this process.

With the task of creating this technology vision in mind, the group brainstormed a list of 60 ideas members believed should be included. After a few people volunteered to create a first draft of the vision, the group adjourned, feeling very productive.

At the next meeting, a draft of the technology vision was presented. The presenters reported that it had been difficult to sift through the ideas and select the most critical components of the vision. Unexpectedly and quickly people locked horns. After 30 frustrating minutes, the senior manager realized what was happening. The task of the group was unclear. They had never agreed on two very important points: (1) What exactly is a technology vision? and (2) How would it be used? Everyone associated with the project was operating under her or his own set of assumptions. They were unable to make progress because they lacked a common understanding of what they were trying to produce.

The senior manager put on her "facilitator's hat" and shared this observation. She then suggested that the group tackle those questions before returning to creating the vision itself. The group responded well to her suggestion. Group members reached consensus on their definition of a technology vision and its use, and afterward were able to refine the technology vision.

By using the facilitator role, the department manager was able to clarify the task early in the project. She got support from the administrator and commitment from the group. In the end, the group produced its technology vision within the 90 days, and the organization was able to put it to good use.

Clarifying the task

One of a facilitator's major responsibilities is helping groups clarify their task before they begin work. The clarifying process may be as quick and simple as making a single statement such as, "My understanding is that the group wants to discuss potential changes to the promotional schedule for the new product launch. Then we'll make decisions about the new schedule."

Usually, however, a facilitator has to do more to ensure that everyone is clear about the task. He or she gathers information from other group members and those issuing the group's assignment. Doing this homework enables facilitators to contribute to the productivity of the people they serve.

The following approaches are useful in helping groups be clear about their task:

1. Check the desired outcome of a meeting at the beginning. *Example:* The facilitator states, "My understanding of the desired outcome of this work session is . . . . How does that compare with your understanding?"
2. Ask clarifying questions. *Example:* The facilitator asks, "What will it look like when the task is successfully completed?"
3. Have the group link the task to the group's overall purpose. *Example:* The facilitator asks, "How will completing this task contribute to completing the project or fulfilling the overall purpose of the group?"

Investing time at the beginning to clarify the task saves time later. In our experience, some groups don't want to spend time clarifying their task because they feel such work is "too process-oriented" or "not enough like real work." Facilitators respond to such statements by asking the group, "How will you know when your task has been fulfilled successfully?" Groups that struggle to answer this question begin to perceive the value in clarifying their task, and most often they choose to do whatever work is necessary to find that answer. Groups that still refuse to clarify their task learn this lesson the hard way.

Establishing a contract between the group and the facilitator

Once the task is clear, the group and facilitator should agree on what they expect from each other. Such expectations can be laid out formally or informally in a contract. The contract does not necessarily have to be in writing, but it should be explicitly discussed. Contracts typically consist of four parts: **task, measures of success, group responsibilities,** and **facilitator responsibilities**. Task is a restatement of the work the group wants to complete. Measuring success is necessary so the group will know when it has completed its task. Differentiating between group responsibilities and facilitator responsibilities helps people determine who will do what to complete the task. Defining responsibilities helps the group and facilitator know what to expect from each other. Contracts might cover as little as one meeting or as much as a wide variety of work over a long period of time.

Figure 1-1 is an example of a simple, one-page contract that a senior management group and its facilitator used to help plan their annual retreat. They decided to use the contract because they had been dissatisfied with the facilitation at the retreat the previous year. The contract helped them have their best retreat.

Figure 1-1   *Sample contract between a group and facilitator*

Facilitator/Group Contract—Annual Planning Retreat

Task	Conduct an effective, efficient planning retreat
Measures of Success	1. Complete next year's business plan 2. Reduce the time to complete the plan by 1 day 3. Identify new sources of sales revenue
Group Responsibilities	1. Confirm purpose and desired outcomes for retreat 2. Confirm facilities and travel logistics 3. Complete prework 4. Approve meeting process 5. Document and distribute retreat proceedings
Facilitator Responsibilities	1. Design retreat process that fulfills purpose and accomplishes desired outcomes 2. Review process with management team prior to retreat; make necessary adjustments 3. Facilitate the work process at the retreat 4. Facilitate debrief meeting and document suggestions for improving next year's retreat

One group member remarked, "When our facilitator first mentioned this contract, I thought, 'Oh no. What is this?' I was afraid it was going to take too much time and yield nothing of use. I was surprised it took only about a half hour to finish the contract. And that one piece of paper sure saved us a lot of time! Last year we dumped all of the documentation work on the facilitator. We ended up losing a lot of information because there was too much for one person to track and record. This year, the contract helped us be more accountable for the retreat outcomes."

Lack of a contract actually bogs down a group and prevents progress. This is ironic because the reason most frequently given for ignoring the contract process is lack of time. Investing time in developing a clear contract between group and facilitator has a very fast payback. The experience of this senior management group with a contract is common: Work is completed faster and more easily.

Contracts help people be clear about roles

What happens when the person who is responsible for facilitating also has managing responsibilities? This is an especially difficult challenge when the group is venturing into an area where the manager does not want them to go. Inappropriately switching from the facilitator to manager role may damage the group's trust and ability to work together effectively. The contract is an excellent tool for identifying these roles and responsibilities. It provides a way to discuss how and when role switches may occur.

At the beginning of this chapter, we defined Task as the work a group needs to complete and stated that tasks exist on more than one level. Effective facilitators use a three-step process—plan, work, and debrief—to help groups complete their tasks. We examine this process in the next section.

Plan, work, and debrief: The general work process for facilitators

No matter how large or small the task, effective facilitators use the same three-step process to help groups get it done: Plan, work, and debrief. This general process is used whether the whole group is meeting or a couple of group members are working together. Step One is to plan the work session. The most important part of this first step is to clarify the task and be clear about what the group wants to accomplish. Step Two is to actually help the group get that work done by following the plan and facilitating the work session. Step Three is to take the time to debrief the work session and determine what worked well and what did not, for both the group and facilitator. This last step usually takes a short time but provides an important evaluation of the work session. By evaluating the effectiveness of the process used to accomplish the work, the facilitator and group learn and improve.

A long-established group in a small pharmaceutical company was working on completing its task of redesigning the marketing strategy for one of the company's products. The whole group met every two weeks for one hour to report progress, make decisions, and plan next steps. The trouble was that everyone had started feeling as though the biweekly meetings were a waste of time. When they got together, everyone assumed they knew what needed to be done. They were all in a hurry to finish so they could get back to other, individual tasks. As a result, they jumped from topic to topic, each person trying to complete what he or she thought was the priority task—but no topic was ever completed before the group was pulled to the next one.

The manager, who was trying to facilitate this meeting, grew weary of trying to keep the group on one topic. When the meeting adjourned, group members demonstrated their frustration by leaving the room quickly. The manager took it upon himself to make up for their lack of progress. He dutifully drafted and circulated minutes of the meeting and completed the tasks he had hoped they would finish. He was working later and later and falling further and further behind.

What was happening here? Group members had never agreed on the purpose of the meetings. They had never planned what they would do. And, they did not have a way to evaluate what they were doing so they could learn and improve.

We suggested the manager use the three-step process for the next meeting: plan, work, and debrief. We suggested allocating five minutes to plan and five minutes to debrief for each hour the group met.

He began the next meeting by clarifying the expected outcomes. The group knew what it was expected to accomplish, and members stayed on topic until the task was finished. Group members were better able to listen and respond because they understood what they were trying to accomplish. For the last five minutes of this meeting, the manager facilitated a discussion of the meeting process. The process of plan, work, and debrief had given the group a new, productive experience. They actually started looking forward to getting together every two weeks.

Focus on task

Effective facilitators always choose their actions to help groups complete their work. Clarifying what people want or need to accomplish always helps produce the results they want. Establishing a contract helps clarify expectations between the group and the facilitator. Every work session, no matter how large or small, begins with a plan and ends with a debrief, so learning and improvement take place.

Effective facilitators are good at helping groups complete their tasks. There is more to facilitation, however, than helping groups efficiently complete their tasks. Groups need a systematic way to organize their work and deliver what their organizations need. We call this systematic approach to getting work done "Charge and Charter."

CHAPTER 2

Clarifying the Charge and Charter of the Group

In this chapter you will learn:

- Why Charge and Charter make such a difference to groups and organizations
- The definition of Charge and Charter
- The elements of Charter: purpose, goals, roles, and procedures
- How to facilitate Charge and Charter

*F*acilitators can use Charge and Charter as a practical way to help groups clarify their overall tasks, organize their work, and get the work done. Identifying and implementing Charge and Charter have a great impact on a group's work.

Charge is the group's overall assignment. The Charge makes clear what is expected of the group. It defines the scope of the work and the results expected. The Charge outlines the obligations of the group to the organization, and it can be measured in some way.

Charter comprises a group's purpose, goals, roles, and procedures. The *purpose* is usually a brief statement outlining why the group exists, whom it serves, and what difference the group's work will make. *Goals* usually are a set of statements that answer the question: What do we need to do to fulfill our purpose? *Roles* define the responsibilities of individuals in the group. Every goal and role must be necessary, and together the set of goals and roles must be sufficient to fulfill the purpose of the group. *Procedures* define how the group will complete its work, both from a social and technical standpoint.

Charge and Charter sets up a dialogue that is focused on getting work done. Being clear about the assignment it has received from the organization helps the group successfully complete its work. Telling the organization how it plans to fulfill the assignment helps the organization know what to expect from the group.

Following are examples of good Charges. Notice that they are concise and measurable.

- The Membership Sales Department will increase its number of members by 8% and increase membership dues revenue by 12% by December 31.
- The Leadership Team will draft a new strategic plan and present it to the Board of Directors for approval by August 15.
- The Product Development Team will scale up the pilot operation to supply 1500 cases of product per month for 12 months, beginning March 21, for a test market in Salt Lake City.

Identifying the Charge

Identifying a Charge is usually quick and easy to do. If the Charge is not already clear, the group asks the following questions of the people responsible for generating it:

1. What are we expected to produce?
2. What will it look like when we are successful?
3. How does this Charge connect with the strategic plan of the organization?

Once a response to each question is generated, one or two sentences are drafted to summarize each answer. These summaries become the Charge.

The process of creating or clarifying a Charge is just as important as the Charge statement itself. Why? Because as they go through this process, those issuing the Charge develop a clear idea of what they are asking a group to do. Developing a Charge is an excellent way to prevent the delivery of "mixed messages" to groups. Leaders who invest as little as 30 minutes to clearly conceive a Charge are better equipped to serve as a resource to the group.

Ideally, a group defines its Charter in response to its Charge. We say ideally because many organizations convene groups without giving them a clear Charge. In some situations, groups are able to elicit a Charge; in others, they are not.

We worked with a new purchasing group in a large corporation that was given the Charge: "Improve the quality of packaging materials coming into our manufacturing plants." Just after the group was formed, the corporation was acquired by another firm. When the manager of the new purchasing group tried to get clarification of the Charge using the three questions above, he received a blunt reply from his boss: "Look, I'll be spending the next 30 days explaining our purchasing contracts to our new senior executives. Your best bet is to make sure your quality improvement initiatives cut costs. I wish I could be more specific, but that is the best I can do right now. As I learn more about our new owners I'll pass it along. For now, you'll have to do the best you can with this assignment." Even though the boss was too busy to formally redefine the Charge, the manager recognized that lowering costs had been added to the original assignment.

In this case, the Charter was a good place for the manager to start helping the new purchasing group get its work done. He immediately facilitated the development of the group's Charter, which outlined a number of short-term and long-term goals for improving quality and cutting costs. Group members then met with major suppliers and enlisted support for fulfilling the Charter. Three weeks later, the group had identified quality improvement initiatives that would generate more than $1 million in annual savings. They were well on their way to completing several projects when the new owners paid their first visit. The new purchasing group was one of the few to avoid major cuts in staffing after the acquisition. Their Charter made the difference.

Helping a group develop its Charter

Figure 2-1 (on page 26) illustrates the elements of a Charter: purpose, goals, roles, and procedures. In groups that use their Charter every day, members carry a copy around with them in a binder. They refer to it often, using it to help them make decisions, plan projects, solve problems, and monitor their progress.

At first glance, developing and using a Charter might seem a bit cumbersome. The process can take time and a lot of work, especially the first few times you do it. With practice, though, people learn to

Figure 2-1   Elements of a group Charter

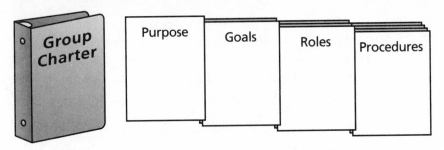

develop a Charter quickly and efficiently. Facilitators who use the process described in the following sections routinely help groups complete their Charter in as little as one day. Groups that use their Charter find it saves them time and helps them be more productive. When an entire organization adopts the Charge and Charter process, the jump in productivity can be astounding.

What do facilitators do to help groups develop each element of their Charter? First, the process usually works best if facilitators develop these elements in the following order:

1. Purpose
2. Goals
3. Roles
4. Procedures

Purpose

A group's purpose statement defines why the group exists, whom it serves, and what difference its work will make to its customers and the organization. Following are guidelines we recommend for developing and using an effective purpose statement:

- Have the group develop the statement so its members feel ownership and understand its meaning.
- Use the statement regularly as an aid to planning, information collection and analysis, problem solving, and decision making.
- State the purpose in 25 words or less, or two concise sentences; don't make it a slogan.

Creating a purpose statement A group should develop its own purpose statement, rather than use one given by someone else. Developing its own purpose statement creates a strong sense of ownership and gives the group a better sense of what it is trying to do—the experience is just as important as the words chosen. Because a group typically struggles over the choice of a particular word or phrase for the statement, those ultimately chosen tend to carry a special meaning to all the members. They feel a stronger sense of commitment about fulfilling the group's purpose because they have helped build it.

An administrative staff at a major university developed this purpose statement: "The purpose of our group is to support faculty and students in their research, teaching, learning, and outreach activities by providing efficient, professional services." They completed this statement during two meetings lasting three hours each. When they shared the statement with their key customers, the response was amazing. For the first time, the faculty members and administrative staff were having conversations about the nature of their working relationship and what they could do to improve it.

Drafting the purpose statement A skilled facilitator can help a group complete its purpose statement quickly, often in as little as two hours. Figure 2-2 (page 28) outlines a process we have used successfully with numerous groups. Working together to discuss and agree upon its overall purpose should be a normal group activity. This process helps.

Do groups always see value in drafting a purpose statement? Often not, because in previous experiences purpose statements (sometimes referred to as "mission statements") were not used after they were created. Effective facilitators frequently ask group members if their work is helping fulfill the group's purpose. By continually relating work and purpose, the facilitator helps the group get a return on its investment in the purpose statement.

Goals

Figure 2-3 (page 29) shows a good goal-setting process. If a group already has a number of goals, the facilitator simply starts with the second step. Any gaps identified during this second step can be filled with a new or modified goal. A group that has done a good job of developing its purpose statement is generally more efficient and

Figure 2-2   *Process for facilitating development of a purpose statement*

Process Step	Facilitator Actions	Questions to be answered in this step
1. Individuals respond to questions 1–3	*Ask individual group members to answer these questions. Questions can be handed out in advance.*	1. What do I believe is the reason this group exists? 2. Who are the primary customers of my group? 3. When my group does its job well, what difference does it make to its customers? The organization?
2. Group listens to all responses	*Ask the group to listen to responses and discuss what they have heard.*	4. What common themes have emerged? 5. Who are all of our customers?
3. Group works to reach consensus on each question	*Ask the group to come up with an answer to each of questions 1–5 in steps 1 and 2.*	
4. Group drafts 1–2 sentence purpose statement	*Ask the group to use the information from step 3 to draft a purpose statement. Use a consensus process like the one here.*	*Consensus Questions:* 1. Can all of you live with this? 2. Will you support it within the group? 3. Will you support it outside of the group? *If one or more group members do not answer yes to Consensus Questions 1–3, then they must answer this question:* What has to change in order for you to support this?

Figure 2-3 *Process for facilitating setting goals*

Process Step	Facilitator Actions	Questions to be answered in this step
1. Group brainstorms possible goals	*Ask the group to brainstorm responses to question 1.*	1. What do we possibly need to do to fulfill our purpose?
2. Group sorts possible goals	*Ask the group to answer questions 2 and 3, first individually and then as a group.*	2. Is this goal necessary? (Consider each goal one at a time. A goal with a "no" answer is discarded.) 3. Is the entire set of goals sufficient to achieve our purpose? If not, what goals must be added?
3. Group prioritizes goals	*Help the group set prioritization criteria from the Charge and purpose. Use multi-voting (see Chapter 7, the tool box) to help the group prioritize its goals.*	4. What criteria are used for prioritizing our goals? 5. Given our prioritization criteria, which goals are most important?
4. Group assigns responsibility and timing for each goal	*Ask the group to assign a member responsibility for each goal.*	6. Who will be responsible for each goal getting accomplished, and when will it be done?

effective in setting goals because the purpose statement serves as a practical guide. A useful format for each goal is as follows:

- *What* exactly should the group do?
- *Who* will be accountable for the completion of this goal?
- *When* must the goal be achieved?

Measures: The key to setting and achieving goals   One of the most important things for groups to do is identify measures that will tell them when they are successfully completing their goals. Groups need to do this regularly; it must become a habit. Failure to measure goals is one of the most frequent causes of group failures. A facilitator can help by frequently asking the group to identify the measures for success: "How will you know when you have achieved this goal?" The answers given by the group identify the measures they need to use.

Figure 2-4 shows some of the goals a customer service group set during its annual planning process. Notice the group identified both the measurement source and the targets for each goal. Goal owners are the individuals in the group accountable for achieving the goal.

Roles

For groups and organizations to get their work done well, they must achieve their goals and fulfill clearly defined roles. This sounds obvious, yet many groups and organizations do a poor job of clearly defining goals and roles. Poorly defined goals prevent a group from delivering results. A person who is unclear about his or her role will be left to guess what he or she is supposed to do, and often will guess wrong. An effective facilitator can identify the signals that indicate an unclear understanding of goals and roles and can take helpful action. Many of those signals are described in Chapter 11.

A group's purpose and goals should be the basis for defining roles. Some groups prefer to define roles before they complete their goals because the group members come from different functional areas of the organization, and members may wish to bring their old job descriptions to their new group. However, this can interfere with the development of a sufficient goal set.

In one situation, a group had just lost a member who had both research and quality assurance duties. The manager in charge of the group was told by the new group member, "I'm from R&D; I know what I am supposed to do, and I'll just do it. There is no need to waste time drawing up a new job description."

The group, however, needed this individual to assume some additional quality assurance responsibilities. The manager and the new group member negotiated around this point for several days, using the group's purpose and goals to help the discussion along. Finally, the

Figure 2-4   Goals from a customer service group's Charter

Goal	Measurement Source and Targets	Goal Owner
Increase customer retention	Source: Sales database • 85% retention (<3 years) • 98% retention (>3 years)	Group manager
Increase customer satisfaction	Sources: Annual survey and customer listening sessions • 4.25 score on Customer Satisfaction Index • Favorable comments from customer listening sessions	Group manager
Improve response time to customer inquiries	Source: Telecom tracking system • Return all calls within 30 minutes. • Respond immediately and accurately on 100% of fax-back requests. • Respond to all written inquiries on the same business day.	Phone and fax operators

new group member agreed to take on some of the quality assurance responsibilities. She was uncomfortable with one of the new duties, though, because she lacked experience with it. The manager then called the group together and facilitated a work session to renegotiate roles within the group. Another group member agreed to take on some of the quality assurance duties and help out the new person as well.

Establishing roles   Figure 2-5 (page 32) shows a good role definition process. Some groups we have worked with have created a detailed description for every role. Others have found that a simple, one-paragraph description meets their needs. Figure 2-6 (page 33) illustrates a role description given in a one-page format that has worked well for a number of groups. It provides sufficient detail to help the group members understand the role, but is not too difficult to draft.

Purpose, goals, and roles are key elements to a group's Charter. They describe who is going to do what to fulfill the purpose of the group. One final element is required to complete the Charter: procedures.

Figure 2-5   Process for facilitating definition of roles

Process Step	Facilitator Actions	Questions to be answered in this step
1. Group brainstorms possible roles	Ask the group to brainstorm responses to questions 1 and 2.	1. What key roles do we need in order to fulfill our purpose? 2. For each role, what skills, knowledge, and abilities are required?
2. Group sorts and assigns roles	Ask the group to answer questions 3 and 4. Then have them assign roles to members by discussing question 5.	3. Is this role necessary? (Consider each role one at a time. A role with a "no" answer is discarded.) 4. Is the entire set of roles sufficient to achieve our purpose? If not, what roles must be added? 5. Who should be assigned to each role?
3. Group defines roles	Help individuals to define their roles. Ask the group to reach consensus on the role definitions.	6. How do I describe my role? 7. What skills, knowledge, and abilities do I think my role requires? 8. How does my role help the group fulfill its purpose? 9. How does my role coordinate with other roles?
4. Group aligns goals with roles	Ask the group to review its set of goals and roles. A matrix sometimes helps this analysis.	10. How do our goals align with our roles?

Figure 2-6 *Role description for a group's accountant*

Group Accountant	As the accountant for the group, I ensure that it meets the financial documentation requirements of both the organization and the IRS. I am responsible for monitoring the group's overall budget and accounts, helping the group stay within the established guidelines. I also act as a liaison between the group and the vice president of finance.
Primary Services	• Project budget monitoring and management • Account budget monitoring and management • Financial document processing • Organizational and IRS compliance
Skills, Knowledge, and Abilities Needed	• CPA credentials • Working knowledge of the organization's accounting and financial management systems • Understanding of the group's Charter • Ability to work well in a team

Procedures

In the context of a group Charter, we define procedures as "how the group will work together." Some procedures, such as ground rules for behavior, are more oriented to group interdependence. Other procedures, such as making decisions, are more oriented to completing activities. In the following discussion, we describe a number of procedures that help groups get their work done. These procedures should be set up in the context of helping the group fulfill its purpose. Group procedures should be compatible with established organizational procedures. They are not meant to replace organizational procedures.

Ground rules for behavior A set of ground rules is the most common procedure we encounter. Such rules call for individuals to respect one another, arrive on time, listen to other ideas, support group decisions, and so on. Generic ground rules handed out to groups by the organization usually do not work. Groups need to generate their own ground rules; otherwise, the rules are less likely to be used. In our experience, we have found an optimal number of ground rules is 10 or fewer.

Group meetings   It is essential that group members agree on the procedure for conducting meetings. The Purpose–Agenda–Logistics format described in Chapter 7 helps groups conduct productive meetings.

Guidelines for communication   We first developed the innovative Purpose–Agenda–Logistics procedure when working with a technology research group and have found it to be very useful. The procedure sets guidelines for using voice mail, e-mail, computer file exchange, and written documents. Because information can be communicated in so many ways, setting standards helps groups be more effective in using those tools available. Following standards contributes to productivity—people know that urgent messages are not buried in an unexpected place. They know what to expect from each other.

Making decisions   Some groups have a hard time making decisions. Thus, it is helpful for groups to have several decision-making procedures available. Groups have successfully incorporated the decision-making process described in Chapter 7 with their Charter.

Experiencing conflict   Responding to conflict is described in Chapter 6. It is extremely helpful for groups to conceive of conflicts as necessary for their health. As such, conflict is something to be managed well; it should not be seen as unproductive interpersonal problems.

Introducing a new group member   Many groups struggle when they need to bring in a new member. Old members often feel too busy to take the time to orient the new member, although this is necessary to help the new member and the group be fully productive. The Charter is an excellent orientation tool for new group members. In addi-

Figure 2-7   Group member experience inventory

Name: _____   Date: _____

Describe one or two of the first jobs you ever had:

Describe the position you held just prior to coming into this group:

List other positions outside of the group you hold now:

List other positions, both inside and outside the organization, you have held:

Describe some key skills you possess that you believe will help the group:

Describe one or more skills you would like to develop in the next six months:

tion, a "Group Member Experience Inventory," such as the one in Figure 2-7, helps the new individual and group get to know one another.

Helping a group member leave smoothly   One of the most disruptive things a group can encounter is the exit of a member. Why? When a member leaves, goals need to be redistributed and roles need to be redefined. Some work won't get done if the group does not do this. The group needs to agree on how it will say good-bye to departing members and address the work that needs to be done. Again, the goals and roles of the Charter provide an excellent management tool for the group to use to minimize this disruption. Because they are written down, goals and roles can more easily be redistributed.

Group procedures are different from the Process element of the Facilitation Model. Group procedures are meaningful mainly in the context of a group's Charter. The Process element of the Facilitation Model refers to more general work processes of groups and what facilitators do to help them.

Let's look again at the university staff that developed a purpose statement. After the good experience of sharing their purpose statement with the faculty, the administrative staff completed the rest of its Charter. In the course of doing so, members learned a lot about themselves as well as the faculty and students they served. The working relationship, which had been rocky between this group and the faculty, was now greatly improved. Most importantly, the group significantly improved its productivity and quality of service. An informal administrative review by the university's central administration revealed that this group had become among the most productive, as measured by the amount of grant money it managed and the number of documents it published.

An architectural firm that had been hired to redesign the administrative staff group's office space used the group's Charter and was able to complete the design in one-third the normal time, thus significantly reducing the costs for this part of the project. When a new administrative assistant to the director was hired, the transition was managed more smoothly than ever before. The group reassigned responsibilities and established a training program to help the new person gain the skills and knowledge needed to fulfill the role. In the past, such changes in personnel had strained relations between faculty and staff as productivity dropped. This time, there was no discernible drop in productivity.

Charge and Charter create accountability

A clearly defined Charge eliminates ambiguity about expectations and makes it easier for a group to figure out what it has to do. Those that issue the Charge are saying to the group, "Here is what we want you to do and why it is important." Further, those that issue the Charge are responsible for it. They must check with the group doing the work and provide feedback about the group's progress.

A good Charter is the group's answer to its Charge. The Charter replies to the issuer of the Charge, "Here is what we think you have asked us to do." A group's Charter improves the odds that the group will deliver against expectations.

The dialogue and work resulting from Charge and Charter help make the group accountable to its customers and the organization. In fact, many groups choose to share part or all of their Charter with their customers. This helps the groups deliver against the expectations of their customers.

One sales group we worked with decided to share its Charter with its biggest customer, a major banking institution. The purchasing agent at the bank helped the sales group adjust its sales goals. In one product category, the bank was phasing out use of a particular model of equipment. In another product category, the bank was planning to purchase more units than the sales group had anticipated. In addition to helping the group adjust its sales quotas, the purchasing agent at the bank suggested that the group make some changes in two key role descriptions. As the group was originally set up, the purchasing agent had to talk to two different members to get her questions answered. She suggested that the group rearrange some duties so that she would have one primary contact. The group agreed and made the changes. As a result, the sales group solidified its relationship with the purchasing agent and is now the preferred supplier with this bank. The Charter was the catalyst for this change.

Charge and Charter provide facilitators with a practical way to help groups get their work done. The various methods used to develop Charge and Charter help groups keep their tasks in focus.

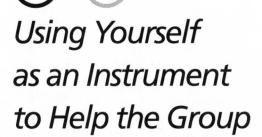

CHAPTER 3

Using Yourself
as an Instrument
to Help the Group

In this chapter you will learn to:

- Be your own best resource
- Be more aware of yourself
- Use your knowledge of yourself to help groups
- Recognize and respond to paradigms
- Consciously choose how to influence others

The most powerful and influential tool effective facilitators bring into a room is themselves. Facilitation is much more than having a bag full of useful tools and activities. Effective facilitators know how to use themselves as an instrument to help groups be more successful. What does it mean to use yourself as an instrument?

First, it means *using your own experience of a group at a particular moment to better understand or question other group members' experiences at that moment.* This is a much richer knowing than simply assuming everyone else is having the same experience. Second, it means using yourself to *model the types of behavior you expect of other group members.* This is a deliberate choice of how you will interact with others so they have concrete examples of the most productive ways to work together.

A new manager in a non-profit organization had met with her staff for the fourth time and she experienced the meetings as continuing to be stiff and formal. In her leader role she had clearly stated her expectation that she and her staff would work collaboratively in an easy, collegial way. She was not yet seeing progress although she was using the facilitator role to create this outcome. During the meetings, she was aware of feeling tension that did not seem associated with the particular agenda items. She believed that if she was feeling that tension, so were the other staff members. The manager knew that the person who had previously held her position had been very directive and did not appreciate people taking positions that differed from hers. Both in and outside of the meetings, the new manager began to explore the expectations of each staff member. Her assumption about why everyone was holding back was confirmed. She stepped back into her leader role by saying, "I need to act as leader for the next few moments," and reaffirmed the new direction. She then consciously modeled the desired new behavior by inviting input from staff and responding positively to what was shared. The staff began to relax and contribute in ways that greatly added to the productivity of the group.

This manager was able to monitor her own reaction to the group meetings. She was curious about how her experience was similar or different from that of the others. She checked her assumptions, confirmed them, and then took constructive action. Without using herself as an instrument to read the group dynamics, she could have easily gotten into a struggle with the group members. They would have dug in their heels if she had tried to force their participation. Instead, she modeled the desired behaviors. Once the source of the tension was revealed, the group learned new ways to interact. The members discovered a way to be more productive.

*K*nowing yourself

Knowing yourself is recognizing your own values, beliefs, needs, perspectives, experiences, and capabilities, and understanding how they affect your facilitation. Each of these has impact on the behavior of facilitators, and the most effective facilitators have taken the time to examine each to better understand themselves.

We define **values** as "what people consider to be important." Effective facilitators value collaboration. They value people and honor differences among them. Facilitators value helping others, building on good relationships to help get the work done. Those who try to facilitate without these values are much more likely to create frustration for themselves and the people with whom they work.

We define **beliefs** as "what people think is true—their reality." An effective facilitator believes he or she is in a supporting role. The facilitator's job is to help the group be the star. The facilitator believes that people function best when they use their individual differences as assets rather than liabilities. The effective facilitator also believes that a group must be clear about its task in order to perform well.

We define **needs** as "what people require to sustain themselves." Everyone has needs that he or she expects the group to satisfy (for example, recognition, achievement, social interaction). Groups may be able to fulfill some of these needs and not others. If facilitators are not aware of these needs, the needs tend to operate as an undercurrent that may detract from the work of the group.

We define **perspectives** as "mental viewpoints used to understand groups." Facilitators' perspectives are created from the merger of their values and beliefs with their experiences and learning. The perspective of a facilitator has a great impact on the meaning he or she makes of what is observed during group interaction. Different meanings lead to different actions by the facilitator.

We define **experiences** as the "series of events participated in or lived through." These events range from the highly successful to the painful failures. Each person's events have individually and collectively affected the way she or he facilitates. Facilitators identify tried-and-true approaches, as well as approaches that will never be tried again. Facilitators benefit greatly from consciously examining their experiences, what they have learned, and how they apply that learning. Some approaches are used too frequently while others may have been abandoned too soon.

We define **capabilities** as "what an individual is able to do." A facilitator's capability may be viewed as three different abilities: (1) the ability to use perspective to glean important information from a group's interactions; (2) the ability to make appropriate meaning of this information; and (3) the ability to act in ways that further the work of the group.

Facilitators who really know themselves act as barometers for their groups. They accurately interpret when their internal experience (being excited, bored, frustrated, angry, and so on) matches that of other group members, a process known as *projection*. Often, acknowledging those feelings to groups enables a group to get unstuck. Facilitators can ask if others feel the same way. This discussion can also give group members permission to share their experiences and feelings, especially if these are different from that of the facilitator.

Facilitators need to resist the temptation to overuse projection, however. Keeping the task in mind helps facilitators gauge how much to use projection. How? If a group is stuck, projecting your feelings about the situation might be helpful. If the group is moving forward with its task, projection might slow it down. Use projection sparingly.

The best facilitators we have trained, observed, and worked with have consistently demonstrated that they valued knowing themselves better. They were willing to reflect on their values, beliefs, needs, perspectives, experiences, and capabilities. They recognized that each of these has had a dramatic impact on how effective they were as facilitators.

Using self-knowledge to drive your behaviors

Facilitators find self-knowledge most useful when it actually helps them become more effective. The real test of the usefulness of this knowledge is whether or not it results in choosing behaviors that help groups be more successful. We define **behaviors** as "what people do that we can observe." Using their knowledge of themselves, facilitators are better able to understand each unique situation and respond appropriately. They are able to better align their intended and actual impact on their groups. Because they can recognize and modify their own behaviors, they are able to help their groups do the same. They can also better choose how to influence the behaviors of the whole group and individual group members.

Intended vs. actual impact

Effective facilitators who are conscious about themselves use all of their resources, more accurately interpret group dynamics, and recognize how groups impact on them. This self-awareness helps them choose helpful actions and model desired behavior. This chapter provides a number of tools facilitators can use to get to know themselves better.

But knowing oneself is not enough to be a good facilitator. Facilitators must also use that self-knowledge to consciously create an *impact on each group*. Of course, facilitators create an impact whether they consciously recognize it or not—and many would be surprised to discover just how different their actual impact is from what they intended. Most facilitators have good intentions about the impact they wish to have. They want to act in ways that are helpful to their groups, but they may be oblivious to the actual elements of their facilitation that create the impact. Facilitators who strive to know themselves are better at creating the impact they want.

A manager, recently assigned to a new group, was frustrated. He knew he needed to act as a facilitator, but he found the role to be very different from what he had been doing before this assignment. Drawing everyone into the conversations proved the hardest part of the role. In the five times the group had met, three of the nine members had been almost totally quiet. They had only responded with a "hello" at the beginning of the meeting and had submitted the written reports that had been requested. The manager wanted these quiet members to be as involved as the rest. He felt the group needed more from them.

The manager sought help from a mentor. As they talked over coffee, the mentor asked about previous experiences the manager had had with quiet group members. The manager remembered a situation years before when someone had been very quiet for months and then one day just exploded. He swore angrily and made demands that the manager leave him alone. The manager had been shocked at the experience. With the mentor's help, the manager realized how the memories of this old situation were causing him to subconsciously worry that one of the current group members might unexpectedly explode on him. He was afraid it would happen again.

The manager could see that he was getting into a struggle with these quiet group members, using his position to try to force participation. At times he had demanded that they make a contribution and had not been satisfied with what they had added. The harder the manager pushed, the more the others pulled back. The manager had been unaware of how much he needed their participation to reassure himself and lessen his fear. By his actions, he was unconsciously sending signals to these members that he was keeping something important from them. In the face of this uncertainty, they protected themselves by remaining quiet.

Using his new awareness, the manager shared his previous experience with the group. He described his fear and asked the quiet group members why they were being quiet. They replied that their style was to keep quiet until they had something of substance to share. He found out they were quite committed to the work of the group. The manager then stated his desire for information to flow more freely and easily within the group. He asked them if they were willing to share before they had something "substantive." Did anything else need to change before they could do that? Several individuals had suggestions, and then the whole group was able to come to an agreement. The behaviors quickly began to change and the group became much more productive.

As this example illustrates, knowing yourself and understanding the difference between intended and actual impact are keys to effective facilitation. Good facilitators are aware of how they are perceived and how their presence influences a group. A critical step for facilitators is coming to understand their own preferences as to how they interact with others. These preferences affect their general orientation, the results they seek, the actions they take to achieve those results, the type of information they need in order to make decisions, and how they determine their own personal value . By understanding their own preferences, facilitators are better able to guard against their own unconscious agendas, which may hinder a group.

Seductive nature of content

One of the most seductive traps for a facilitator is being drawn into participation in the content of a group's discussion. This is especially true when the facilitator has expertise and experience with the subject at hand. Listening intently to a conversation and actively drawing others into the discussion often leads a facilitator to want to add his or her "two cents' worth." Participating in a discussion in this way is part of the manager and leader roles but not of the facilitator role. Facilitators can be most effective when they remain neutral. If the facilitator also has a manager or leader role and wishes to contribute, an obvious switch of roles is necessary. Knowing one's own agenda is critical to making these choices and in being able to shift roles smoothly.

The concept of paradigms

The *concept* of paradigms can help facilitators better understand their role in assisting groups to be successful. During the early 1990s, the *word paradigm* was overused and poorly understood. In many cases, the word was—and still is—associated with failed reorganizations. For now, we ask you to suspend any negative feelings you have about the word and focus on the concept. When facilitators are conscious of their own paradigms, they can more easily understand and positively influence the groups they serve.

Very simply, paradigms tell us what information to consider important and how to use that information to solve problems. They make it easier to sort through the overwhelming amount of information that bombards us each day. Paradigms function as a spotlight in a dark room. They illuminate some information while leaving other information in the dark. Because this illumination process tends to be automatic, outside everyone's awareness, it is important for facilitators to recognize the paradigms they are using so they can be alert to important information that may be in the shadows cast by these paradigms.

A facilitator who values getting work done quickly and assumes the group needs a lot of direction will facilitate in a very active, take charge manner. This contrasts with a facilitator who feels it is most important for a group to learn primarily through its own experiences and needs only well-timed nudges to stay on track. This facilitator will be more of an observer, who acts by being more inviting than directive. These two facilitators have very different facilitation paradigms.

Each facilitator has his or her own paradigm for facilitation. This is the paradigm that has been learned from participating in and with groups, working with other facilitators, attending workshops and classes, and reading. Each individual's paradigm is unique. A facilitator's paradigm supports or inhibits the facilitator's ability to do his or her job.

Paradigms defined

Thomas Kuhn, who wrote the classic work on paradigms, examined the concept and made discoveries that are helpful to facilitators. He found that paradigms had four elements: **behaviors/activities, vocabulary, assumptions/beliefs,** and **values.** Table 3-1 (page 46) defines these elements. The examples show the kinds of obvious changes that have to be made with each element in order for a group to function collaboratively.

We pay most of our attention to behaviors and activities because these can be seen. Vocabulary, assumptions/beliefs, and values are

Table 3-1 *Elements of a paradigm*

	Definition	*Examples*
Behaviors/ Activities	Those worked-out approaches and solutions that display the world view as a coherent whole	Structured discussion to gain everyone's input rather than announcing directions
Vocabulary	The words that are used to communicate; how problems are posed and solutions described	The new behavior must have a new name: "collaborative problem solving" rather than "following orders"
Assumptions/ Beliefs	Those taken-for-granted beliefs about what is real or true; the foundation for the behaviors and activities that are chosen	People make choices about their own changes rather than having people change when they are forced to change
Values	The expression of what is important; these become the basis for setting priorities and making choices of what goals to pursue and problems to solve	People's ability to make choices about their own lives must be respected rather than having management's perspective always take precedence

not usually discussed, so we are much less aware of their effect on ourselves and others. The more often that people have found that their current paradigm successfully solves their most critical problems, the harder it is for them to identify and discuss the paradigm itself. Under these conditions, the paradigm is simply taken for granted and becomes invisible. For individuals and groups whose current paradigm is less able to solve the most critical problems, the limits of the paradigm are more apparent. It is easier for them to identify the behaviors/activities, vocabulary, assumptions/beliefs, and values associated with their paradigm.

Organizations that attempt to change their paradigm but focus their change efforts only on behaviors and activities are doomed to failure. This is also true for groups attempting to operate differently from the ways they did in the past. The continued use of the vocabulary, assumptions/beliefs, and values of the old paradigms will undermine the use of the new behaviors, and the old paradigms will soon be back in place.

Your own paradigms

You will improve your skills as a facilitator by examining your own paradigm for facilitation. Ask yourself, "What behaviors will help me fulfill this role? What words do I use when I ask a group to clarify its task? What do I believe is true about this group? Do I really believe that the group should be the star?" Once you evaluate your own facilitation paradigm, you can better help the group look at its paradigms. A group that is aware of its existing paradigms is better able to make changes.

A practical way to evaluate your own facilitation paradigm is to construct a table similar to Table 3-1. Write down some of your own facilitation behaviors, vocabulary, assumptions/beliefs, and values. Identify changes you will need to make to these paradigm elements in order to improve your facilitation skills. The more you understand your own paradigm, the better able you will be to use yourself as a barometer for what is happening with others in the group. You will also be better prepared to help individuals and groups identify and change their paradigms.

Consider the experience of a faculty group at a medical research institute. This group was experiencing major changes: (1) They were suddenly competing with for-profit clinics for patients and research grants. (2) They were being asked to add management responsibilities to their jobs. And (3) their major source of funding, the state legislature, was putting new, aggressive performance demands on them.

As part of their change process, this group was asked to define its current and future paradigms. The group discovered that it used negative vocabulary to describe management activities: "bean counting" and "the opposite of research." Members believed that performing management duties was a step down for them. However, the reality was that they would have to adopt some management responsibilities or get closed down. Some of them decided to revisit their assumptions and beliefs about management duties. They tried to redefine management as a skill they had to master. If they could get more efficient at management, they would have more time to do the work they truly loved: medical research.

Creating new paradigms

Facilitators can help groups achieve breakthrough performances by calling attention to the paradigms they use and helping them create new ones. The first challenge is for a group to agree that it might be possible to dramatically improve its performance. If members believe they are already at a superior level of performance, they will consider their paradigm highly successful and have no need to make a change.

We have an exercise where small groups are timed as they pass three tennis balls around. The groups usually feel very good when they complete the task within 15 seconds. They always accept the challenge to complete the task faster and usually shave another second or two off their time. When asked if they have achieved the optimal time, they say they are close but might be able to do a little better. When told that other groups have done it in less than 5 seconds, they are at first shocked. Then they clarify their task again, reassess how they have completed it, try radically different approaches, and successfully reduce the time to under 5 seconds. The groups question their assumptions and beliefs during this exercise. Until they do this, they cannot conceive of the approaches they will soon successfully use. Their behaviors cannot really change until their assumptions/beliefs change.

Generally, people are so focused on whatever they are doing that they do not step back and reflect on their paradigms. Facilitators are in a unique position to help groups take the time to do this. Often the best place to start is by helping groups identify the underlying assumptions and beliefs that guide their work. When groups take this task seriously, they can quickly come to new understandings about the ways they work together. Once the assumptions/beliefs are identified, they can be vigorously challenged. Finding new behaviors that fit a new set of assumptions/beliefs is then a much easier task.

Influencing each other

As facilitators, we must understand many basics about human behavior. One key area is how people influence each other. We have all attempted to exert our influence over others and have experienced having others try to influence us. According to researchers such as B. F. Skinner and Albert Bandura, there are four fundamental methods for influencing the behavior of others: positive reinforcement, punishment, negative reinforcement, and extinction. These are described in detail in Table 3-2.

Our experience with influencing

Facilitators often work hard to influence the behavior of individuals in their groups. The strange irony is that frequently the facilitators are influencing the behaviors—but not in ways they had expected or intended. If facilitators do not consciously think about this influencing process, the influence they do exert may not produce the desired results.

In the example in Table 3-2 (page 50), the facilitator was practicing **positive reinforcement** when saying "good idea" in response to contributions during a brainstorming session. This type of verbal reinforcer tends to encourage the person being reinforced to contribute again. Many responses can function as a positive reinforcer. Body language, such as a smile or nodding the head, is frequently used. The primary emotion experienced in response to positive reinforcement is pleasure.

But, what happens when the "good idea" does not occur with every contribution? If only a few people receive it, they are the only ones reinforced. The others may feel slighted. They may choose to refrain from contributing in the future so they do not experience the slight again. They are experiencing **negative reinforcement** in that they are taking action to avoid a negative experience. No longer experiencing the slight reinforces not making contributions. Emotionally, the primary response to negative reinforcement is disengagement. People stop caring. If only some ideas are reinforced and others are simply noted or even ignored, positive reinforcement has been used, in a particular way, to guide the attention of the group and even the outcome

Table 3-2   Methods of influencing

Method	Definition	How Long the Behavior Lasts	Example
Positive Reinforcement	When the desired behavior occurs, a reward is received. The individual receiving the reward associates it with a particular behavior and, if the reward is valued, tends to repeat the behavior.	Behavior learned this way is most likely to endure. The learning is most powerful if the behavior is intermittently reinforced.	During a discussion, a group leader says "good idea" in response to a contribution.
Punishment	When an undesired behavior occurs, an undesirable consequence is received. The individual receiving the punishment associates it with a particular behavior and tends not to repeat the behavior as long as the threat of punishment persists.	Behavior learned this way is likely to continue only so long as there is an expectation of further punishment.	During a discussion, a group leader ridicules a group member's contribution.
Negative Reinforcement	Behavior occurs with the intent of eliminating unwanted circumstances or actions. Because something has previously happened, the individual takes some form of action to prevent it from happening again.	Behavior learned in this way is likely to endure, unless the unwanted circumstances or situation reappears.	A group member avoids making contributions so he or she will not be ridiculed.

Table 3-2 *Methods of influencing (continued)*

Method	Definition	How Long the Behavior Lasts	Example
Extinction	When a particular behavior that is expected to be rewarded is not, the individual vior will occur less frequently and will eventually no longer be exhibited.	Behavior will become less frequent until it disappears, unless it is again rewarded.	A group member stops trying to contribute when she or he is ignored.

of the discussion. Such behavior may be unconscious to the facilitator, but can have a dramatic influence on a group.

Punishment is experienced as a very specific act. Although the word *punishment* often creates images of "being taken out to the woodshed," it is practiced in groups in much more subtle ways. Punishment is an overt use of power in a group. Punishment usually is intended to control the behavior of others. It assumes that people are not able to control their own behavior so that they act in predetermined ways. Punishment is intended to "get them back in line." It demonstrates that one person has more or less power than another. The example used in Table 3-2—ridiculing a member's contribution—is a common form of punishment within groups. But there are many others, including body language. Rolling of the eyes or a big frown can cause an immediate reaction. Individuals may be assigned undesirable tasks because of something they did or said. The most common emotions experienced in response to punishment are fear and/or anger. Frequent use of punishment creates an environment where it is very difficult for group members to collaborate or even get their work done.

Extinction is experienced less frequently, but it can have a powerful effect on behavior. Many groups have members who tend to be ignored by both the rest of the group and by the facilitator. Phrases such as "no one listens to me in that group," "it doesn't make a difference to the group whether I'm there or not," or "I'm tired of trying to get their attention" should be red flags for a facilitator. Valuable contributions are being lost. Effective facilitators are expected to find ways to include all group members. This means structuring work sessions so it is easier for all group members to contribute. For instance, giving group members time to work silently helps those who work better alone.

Research indicates that positive reinforcement has the longest lasting effect of all the influences. People adopt behaviors that have led to good results. Punishment affects our behavior only when we fear the punishment and believe there is a real chance of being caught. Groups who constantly experience fear of something bad happening to them tend to protect themselves. They are less likely to be risk takers. Facilitation, however, is about creating an atmosphere of trust and risk taking. Positively reinforcing group members for working together and challenging the status quo creates an environment where groups can break old paradigms and find success in new and exciting ways.

Self as instrument

Learning more about yourself is the most productive activity you can do to improve your ability to facilitate. Better appreciation of the impact of your values, beliefs, needs, perspectives, experiences, and capabilities prepares you to respond more effectively in every facilitation situation. Knowing yourself helps you recognize your own paradigms, modify them if appropriate, and help your group address its paradigms. Awareness of how you interact with group members will lead you to consciously use different approaches to influencing that help your group be more successful. This prepares you and your group to productively use differences among group members. It is in capitalizing on the differences that groups can really excel.

Benefiting from Individual Differences

In this chapter you will learn to:

- Recognize and appreciate differences
- Recognize and respond to styles
- Help groups utilize their differences

Differences among individuals

Each person experiences others and the world in a unique way. We know that some people are more like us and some are quite different. Some people tend to focus on details, while others only want to look at the "Big Picture." Some operate more as outgoing, impatient, and risk taking, whereas others are quieter, patient, and more cautious. Some focus more on facts and the task, whereas others focus more on people.

Since the ancient Greeks identified four temperaments (choleric, sanguine, phlegmatic, and melancholic), students of human behavior have been categorizing people on this basis. People differ in how outgoing or patient they are. They may tend to take or avoid risks. They may be more task-oriented or people-oriented. Understanding these patterns provides facilitators with additional tools for understanding both themselves and the members of a group they are facilitating.

Groups need a variety of behavioral styles in order to perform at their best. It is from diversity that the richest, most productive ideas arise. One group member may think of an idea and then others can build on it. Because they are not alike, group members have different concerns and are often better at completing different types of tasks. The most productive groups have memberships that reflect a balance of various behavior preferences.

The very differences that lead to higher productivity also can lead to painful conflict. We tend to have the most problems with people who have different behavior patterns from our own. We experience the world so differently that we often tend to see "them" as a problem. "If only they would be more like me!" But if they were—no matter how wonderful the "me" was—the others would simply be clones. It would not be possible to build on each other's work.

Facilitators need to be aware of how they and others operate and be able to appreciate and use these differences. If differences among group members are not experienced as a strength, they may be seen as a problem. In this case, facilitators may have missed an opportunity to draw on the differences as resources.

There are a number of instruments that facilitators can use to help them understand behavioral differences. These instruments provide a simple assessment of individual behavior preferences. Some are self-administered, including a self-scoring questionnaire and explanatory materials. Most, however, are designed to be used in conjunction with a trained specialist, who helps individuals and groups use the information appropriately. To help facilitators gain the most from using such instruments, we recommend they work with a specialist.

Although each instrument describes human behavior a little differently, facilitators need to use the descriptions consistently. The following observations about behavior preferences apply to any instrument:

- *Everyone has a preference for one or more styles.* The preferred style is the first choice. If current or past experience indicates the preferred style is less effective, then a back-up style is used. Various instruments identify the degree to which different styles are preferred.
- *Everyone has the capability to demonstrate a variety of styles.* People respond to different situations by altering which style is used.
- *People view the world from their style tendencies.* Unless they consciously accept differences, people usually expect others to operate as they do. Others may be viewed as "wrong" if they differ.

- *There is no right or wrong style.* No style is more or less important or correct than others. Particular styles may be more or less effective in specific situations.
- *Each style has strengths and weaknesses.* The strength of one style is the weakness of another style. People with different style preferences have much to teach each other.

More specific material on identifying and using differences in behavior styles is presented in the following sections. We suggest that facilitators use this material to help them get to know themselves better and to recognize the preferences of others. This knowledge is a rich resource for facilitators who are seeking to help their groups be more successful. A variety of instruments is available (see the Instruments list at the end of the book). We have found the DISC model (introduced in the next section) to be an easy-to-use approach, and many organizations already use some system based on this model. We have also found the Jung-based systems to be useful. They provide information on more continuums than the DISC and are popular with many organizations.

Introduction to the DISC description of styles

One of the most common approaches to identifying behavioral style differences is the DISC model. It is based on the Greek categorization of temperaments, previously mentioned, but has been refined by numerous people, especially in the last 50 years. A number of authors, such as Geier and Merrill and Reid have expanded on earlier descriptions. The model provides general descriptions of the preferences people exhibit—not detailed psychological assessments. Many people, in a wide variety of settings, have found these descriptions to be helpful in better appreciating and benefiting from differences.

The DISC approach provides a way of describing people's preferences. It measures these using two continuums: Assertiveness and Responsiveness. Depending on a person's position on these continuums, he or she will be identified as having a preference for one of four behavior patterns. The continuums are depicted in Figures 4-1 and 4-2 (page 56). The assertiveness continuum reflects the willingness and ability of people to share their ideas, needs, and desires. The responsiveness continuum reflects the willingness and ability of people to share or display their feelings.

Figure 4-1   Assertiveness continuum

High Assertive

High assertive people speak up forcefully and initiate social interactions. They present their positions with confidence.

Low Assertive

Low assertive people are more likely to seek information by asking questions and then listening. They appear quieter, more easygoing.

Figure 4-2   Responsiveness continuum

Low Responsive  **High Responsive**

Low responsive people are less ready to communicate their feelings. They appear to be more concerned with controlling situations, and may seem indifferent to others while they focus on achieving results.

High responsive people appear to be influenced by events and other people. They more readily express their anger, joy, and sadness. They are more focused on being accepted by others.

Style preferences as described by DISC

When these two continuums are put together, we can see that people have distinctly different preferences in how they experience other people and events. The combined continuums are the basis for the four behavior styles, described in Figure 4-3.

Individuals who prefer to act in a high assertive and low responsive way have been described as drivers. They seek *dominance* and are the *D* in DISC. They tend to use the words *I* and *me* most often. The objective of much of their communication is to give people information or to tell them what to do. When engaged in conflict, they seek to win, even at another's expense. People who prefer a **Dominance** style tend to be more direct, decisive, independent, and results-oriented. In interacting with people, they tend to be positive and

Figure 4-3 Style preferences when the continuums are put together

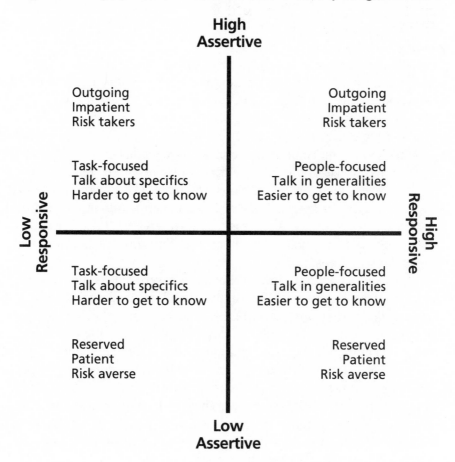

straightforward. They are often seen as inquisitive, competitive, willing to take risks, and adventuresome. They are also experienced as hasty, overly aggressive, disparaging, and insensitive.

Those who prefer to act in a high assertive and high responsive way have been described as enthusiastic. They seek to *induce* or influence others and are the *I* in DISC. They tend to use the words *we* and *us* most often. Their communication objective is to sell ideas or plans. When faced with conflict, they seek to win but want others to embrace the solution. People who prefer an **Inducement** style tend to be enthusiastic, persuasive, confident, and influential. In interacting with people, they tend to be charming, poised, and sensitive. They are often seen as impulsive, generous, optimistic, and wanting to work with others. They also may be experienced as self-promoting, unrealistic, willing to trust people indiscriminately, and not willing to consider the facts when making decisions.

High responsive people who are also low on the assertive continuum are described as social or amiable. They seek *steadiness* in their lives and are the *S* in DISC. They are more likely to use the word *you* when communicating. In dealing with conflict, they often accommodate, letting others have their way. People who prefer a **Steadiness** style tend to be self-controlled, amiable, more predictable, and patient. In interacting with people, they tend to be reserved, relaxed, and develop deep, long-lasting relationships. They like to work in small, familiar groups or teams. They are often seen as having unending patience when following a process they have accepted. They also may be experienced as unwilling to change the status quo, overly cautious, dependent, and possessive.

Individuals who are low on both the assertiveness and responsiveness continuums are often experienced as more analytical and *conscientious*. They are the *C* in DISC. They are more likely to expect written communications with sufficient detail to prove the points presented. They do not like conflict and look for ways to avoid it. People who prefer a **Conscientious** style tend to be industrious, analytical, systematic, and patient. In interacting with people, they tend to be reserved, diplomatic, and sensitive. They are often seen as adaptable, precise, discrete, factual, and concerned with quality. They also may be experienced as overly perfectionistic, indecisive, narrowly focused, and likely to withdraw when threatened.

It is important to note that there are no good or bad preference patterns. Each preference pattern has inherent strengths and weaknesses. People with different preference patterns believe differently, think differently, and act differently. They see and hear very different information. They experience the world in fundamentally different ways. Facilitators must look to people with different preference patterns as necessary resources for each group.

Strengths and weaknesses for facilitation

Facilitators may prefer any of the four styles and still be successful. A preference for any particular style creates both strengths and weaknesses for a facilitator, as described in Table 4-1. Part of the skill of an

Table 4-1   Strengths and weaknesses of each style for facilitators

	Strengths	Weaknesses
D **Dominance** **Directing**	May tend to: • Focus on desired outcome • Be direct and decisive • Be positive and confident • Be willing to take risks	May tend to: • Talk too much • Control the direction and process of group • Be blunt and sarcastic • Be insufficiently patient
I **Inducement** **Influencing**	May tend to: • Be enthusiastic • Want to include everyone • Be willing to take risks • Be charming and poised	May tend to: • Talk too much • Act impulsively, counter to the facts • Jump to inconsistent conclusions • Attend insufficiently to details
S **Steadiness** **Stabilizing**	May tend to: • Be quieter and more patient • Persist until goals are reached • Create a warm and predictable group atmosphere • Foster cooperation and teamwork	May tend to: • Not adjust quickly to changes in the group • Be unwilling to change his or her facilitation process • Have trouble balancing several tasks • Be upset by open conflict situations
C **Conscientious** **Complying**	May tend to: • Be very task-oriented • Approach problems in a systematic way • Be diplomatic in interactions with group members • Attend to achieving a high-quality outcome	May tend to: • Be unwilling to address emotional content of interactions • Avoid conflict • Be bound by accepted procedures and methods • Be less willing to take risks and act without sufficient precedent

effective facilitator is to take advantage of the strengths and compensate for the weaknesses. Because everyone has the ability to operate from any of the four styles, effective facilitators can usually shift styles to match the needs of their groups. Their style flexibility is achieved because they are aware of their own style preferences and use their knowledge of these style choices to shift appropriately.

Facilitators, as noted, need to understand both their own behavior preferences and those of others. The behavior of group members reflects their style preferences. Knowing these preferences allows facilitators to modify their own behavior to have the most positive impact on the group. Tables 4-2 through 4-5 list common behavioral cues that facilitators can use to create sound, educated guesses concerning the preferences of others.

Using style information with groups

Facilitators do not necessarily need to use an instrument to identify style preferences. Unique combinations of behaviors are associated with each of the four styles, and observing the behavior patterns of individuals can provide important clues about their style preferences. Some individuals are easy to place in one of the four types. Many others exhibit some of two or more preferences. Do these individuals tend to use a particular preference in a particular situation? Once facilitators know how to better respond to the various preferences, they can adjust their behavior to each situation. Choice of behavior should be driven by a facilitator's desire to help a group complete its work and interact more effectively.

Awareness of preferences is not a form of psychoanalysis or manipulation. Such awareness helps facilitators to be more conscious of the behaviors of group members and make the best choices for responding to them. It allows them to make better choices about how to help groups be more successful.

Once facilitators have identified the style preferences of individuals in a group, they can better understand members' perspectives, actions, emotions, and needs. Accepting these as preferences—and not absolutes—prevents the individuals from being "pigeonholed." Facilitators are simply being more systematic in responding to the individual differences that occur in every group.

Table 4-2 Working with people who have the Dominance style

Recognize them when they:
- Speak faster, louder, and with less inflection
- Tend to make more statements and ask fewer questions
- Prefer to focus on facts or task

What upsets them?
- Telling them what to do
- Attacking their character
- A situation where they might lose
- Inaction

How you can influence them:
- Be brief and get to the point quickly.
- Provide concise answers that address a narrow view of the question.
- Agree with facts and ideas rather than the person, when in agreement.
- Outline alternatives that can lead to success; make recommendations, but allow them to make a choice, when in disagreement.
- Stress all the benefits you can, but be prepared to support your claims.
- Stress what is in it for them.

Table 4-3 Working with people who have the Inducement style

Recognize them when they:
- Speak faster, louder, and with more inflection
- Tend to ask more questions and make more statements
- Prefer to focus on opinions and stories

What upsets them?
- Avoiding or rejecting them
- Denying their acceptance and friendship
- Being negative about their ideas
- Isolation

How you can influence them:
- Offer them suggestions for transferring their ideas to concrete action.
- Provide testimonials of others on ideas or plans.
- Tell stories about how others have successfully used the ideas or plans.
- Provide details in writing but do not dwell on them.
- Provide incentives for taking on tasks.
- Ask direct questions and let them explain themselves.
- Suggest alternative solutions you both can explore and create.

Table 4-4   Working with people who have the Steadiness style

Recognize them when they:
- Speak more slowly, softer, and with more inflection
- Tend to make fewer statements and ask more questions
- Prefer to focus on opinions and stories

What upsets them?
- Overlooking or confusing them
- Sudden, unplanned, risky changes
- Competition rather than cooperation
- Conflict situations

How you can influence them:
- Focus on answers to *how* questions to provide them with clarification.
- Provide ideas or departures from current practices in a nonthreatening manner; give them a chance to adjust; don't push for agreement too quickly.
- Clearly define goals, roles, or procedures and their place in the overall plan.
- Provide assurances of follow-up support.
- Emphasize how their actions will minimize risks involved and enhance current practices.
- Take a sincere, personal interest in their well-being.

Table 4-5   Working with people who have the Conscientious style

Recognize them when they:
- Speak more slowly, softer, and with less inflection
- Tend to make fewer statements and ask fewer questions
- Prefer to focus on facts or task

What upsets them?
- Criticizing their effort or ideas
- Asking personal or blunt questions
- Incomplete or inaccurate recommendations
- Expecting them to become emotionally or personally involved

How you can influence them:
- Provide straight pros and cons of ideas.
- Support ideas with accurate data.
- Provide assurances that no surprises will appear.
- Review recommendations to them in a systematic and comprehensive manner.
- Be specific, if agreeing.
- Disagree with the facts rather than the person, if disagreeing.
- Be prepared to provide explanations in a patient, persistent, diplomatic manner.

Tables 4-2 through 4-5 describe each of the four style preferences. The tables can help facilitators recognize and work more effectively with each style. People that we have trained report that these charts are practical, helping them facilitate more effectively.

An alternative approach to personality differences

An alternative approach to the DISC model for identifying and better understanding differences is based on the work of Carl Jung. Instruments also have been developed to utilize this system. Examples are the Myers-Briggs Type Inventory® (MBTI®) and the Keirsey Temperament Sorter. This approach identifies personality types. It places individuals within one of four categories, based on how they are energized, gather information, make decisions, and prioritize gathering information or making decisions (see Table 4-6).

The preferences in each category are reflected by the letters used to describe them: ESTP, INFJ, ENTJ, and so on. Because there are four different continuums, there are 16 different letter combinations. Each combination represents a different preference pattern. Additional information about this approach is available. (See the Instruments list at the end of the book.)

Table 4-6   Jungian-based personality styles

Extravert–Introvert E ├────────┤ I	Gains energy by being with groups of people (E) or by being alone or with a few people (I)
Sensing–Intuitive S ├────────┤ N	Gathers information based on the senses (S) or assumes there is more behind what was sensed (N)
Thinking–Feeling T ├────────┤ F	Makes decisions based on logic (T) or on feelings/values (F)
Perceiving–Judging P ├────────┤ J	Focuses on gathering information (P) or making decisions (J)

Benefiting from differences

Groups, of course, can benefit from differences among members whether the differences are categorized by one of the preceding systems or not. Groups that describe their differences in a positive way are in a better position to capitalize on them, and are less likely to experience the differences as irritations or serious problems. The systems just described provide a positive perspective on differences.

Facilitators who are aware of their own preferences know themselves better. They understand the strengths and weaknesses of their preferred styles, and they know how to shift to alternative styles when that would be more helpful to their groups. Also, knowing more about their own preferences helps facilitators better understand how others experience situations and helps them decide which action to take. This understanding is an important foundation to discovering more about group dynamics.

CHAPTER 5

Understanding Group Interaction and Development

In this chapter you will learn:

- Why group histories are helpful
- How to use the 'Orming Model
- About the Group Development Curve
- How to observe and interpret
- How rank ordering of systems impacts groups

*E*ffective facilitators understand and encourage improvement of group dynamics. They know how to use their presence to help a group accomplish its task and become more productive. They help a group capitalize on conflict rather than be disabled by it. The facilitators we have trained and supported have reported dramatic performance improvements by their groups from using the practical approach to managing conflict outlined in Chapter 6.

Effective facilitators recognize which behaviors in groups are normal parts of group interaction and which are problems to be addressed. This chapter prepares facilitators to make these assessments and take productive action. It describes the impact of history on groups, stages of group formation and adjustment, types of groups, and group relationship styles.

Group history

When a facilitator works with a group for the first time, it is important that she or he understand the context in which this entrance is occurring. Even newly formed groups have some form of history that will affect their functioning. Systematically gathering this information will help a facilitator understand why the group behaves in certain ways.

The list of questions in Figure 5-1 helps facilitators find out more about groups. They should ask these questions when they are first assigned to a group. The group and the person who assigned them are good resources for the answers. The process of asking these questions often helps a facilitator connect more quickly with a group. The questions do not need to be answered in any particular order. The most interesting part of the process is to see where the responses lead. It is also revealing to see the range of different responses. Exploring the group's history prepares facilitators to better understand the behaviors they observe and make better choices about how they will interact with the group.

Figure 5-1   *Group history questionnaire*

Group History Questionnaire
- Why was the group formed?
- How long ago was the group formed?
- Has membership in the group changed significantly since it was formed? If so, how has it changed? For what reasons did people leave? What was the impact of their leaving?
- Has membership in the group changed significantly in the past year? If so, how has it changed?
- To whom is the group now accountable? How is that accountability experienced?
- What are examples of successes the group has achieved?
- What are examples of goals or objectives the group has been unable to meet?
- How has leadership emerged within the group?
- How have plans been developed by the group?
- What processes have the group developed to help them work together?
- How has conflict been experienced by the group?
- Have facilitators who have not been group members or leaders worked with this group? What was the group's experience of the facilitator?
- How is the group's culture similar and different from the culture of the larger organization?
- How is the group organized? Has the group developed an organizational chart?

Working together

Productive groups are not magically created by bringing together a collection of individuals. Without intentional effort to create a group, the results are unpredictable. Nearly everyone can remember a grouping of people that did not come together well. They were always less productive than expected. In many of these situations, the groups did not consciously try to develop. Instead, they rushed into working on their Charge, their assigned task, and their haste left them ill prepared to fulfill the Charge.

To be productive, groups must complete work related to each of four stages: **Forming, Storming, Norming,** and **Performing.** The stages were first described by Bruce Tuckman in the 1960s. We refer to them as the **'Orming Model** (see Figure 5-2). Each stage requires attention and conscientious action. Effective facilitators help groups understand that working through the tasks associated with each stage is "real work"—vital to the successful completion of the group's Charge.

When first working with groups, facilitators should determine the current stage of the group. Then they should help the group understand where it is, how it got there, and how it can progress to the next stage. As the group becomes more adept at identifying its current stage, it will increase its interpersonal effectiveness, improve its

Figure 5-2 'Orming Model

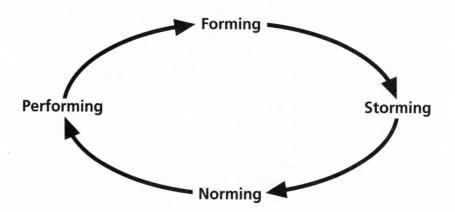

performance, and move through the other stages at a more efficient pace. Tables 5-1 through 5-4 summarize the nature of each stage and the practical work that needs to be completed before the group can move to the next stage.

Groups—whether formal teams, work groups, or temporary groups —need to evolve through these four stages. By completing the specific tasks for each stage, a group becomes more cohesive and productive more quickly. Facilitators contribute to productivity by explaining the need to work through the stages, offering ways to complete the work, and then supporting the group's results. This is an especially important part of the facilitator's role because groups may tend to get stuck in the Forming, Storming, or Norming stages and thus fail to reach their full potential.

Any time a group experiences changes in membership or leadership, completes a major assignment, or gains a new assignment, it will

Table 5-1 Forming	
Work to be done	*Understand the purpose* of the group and who are the other group members.
	This often looks like: *restating the Charge* to the group, *introducing* group members, *assessing the resources* each member brings, *participating* in activities to experience the skills, knowledge, and work styles of the others.
Behaviors and dynamics that may be observed	• Uncertainty regarding purpose and goals • Introductions • Socially oriented behavior • Enthusiasm • Tentativeness • Testing behavior • Feelings of anxiety • Needing to find a place in the group
Questions to be answered	• Why are we here? • Who are these people?
Problems that will continue to surface if not addressed	• People going in different directions • People not recognizing the people resources within the group

Table 5-2   Storming

Work to be done	*Identify what individuals expect* from each other and *how they expect to work together.* This often looks like: opportunities to state *expectations, identification of differences,* and *experiences of conflict.*
Behaviors and dynamics that may be observed	• Conflict, both within and outside of group • Uncertainty about roles • Possibly overzealous interactions • Strong resistance to group formation • Frustration • Discrepancy between hopes and reality • Competition • Possible formation of cliques
Questions to be answered	• What do I expect from others? • What do they expect from me?
Problems that will continue to surface if not addressed	• People getting upset because their expectations are not being met • People feeling they are having to do too much of the work • People feeling they are not an important or useful part of the group

cycle through the four stages again. If a group has learned this process, it will be able to cycle through each stage much more quickly. The group will have learned an important skill: adapting to change while maintaining productivity. Facilitators provide an important service to groups by helping them use this process to their advantage, rather than experiencing the problems inherent in ignoring it.

Nature of groups

We define the productivity of all groups in terms of their performance and their interdependence. Attending to both performance and interdependence allows groups to break through the "productivity limit"—the cumulative work done by each group member working individually.

Table 5-3   Norming

Work to be done	*Resolve differences* in what members expect of each other and how they will work together. This often looks like: *establishing ground rules* and *preparing the group's Charter,* which will spell out how the group works together.
Behaviors and dynamics that may be observed	• Negotiation • Identifying commonly held purpose • Forming group spirit • Group beginning to work together • Members supporting leadership and each other • Group oriented to accomplishing mutual goals • Harmony, trust, and respect developing
Questions to be answered	• How are we going to work together?
Problems that will continue to surface if not addressed	• Group members not agreeing on how they will work together • Group members working at cross-purposes with other group members

Groups are usually created to increase productivity in an organization, complete a particular project, and/or improve an organizational process. They are created because there are practical limits on the quantity and quality of work an individual can produce working alone. No matter how many times people are told to "work smarter," they will eventually hit the limit of the work they can produce. Likewise, a group that has little or no sense of its building on the work of group members will experience a limit on the amount and quality of work it can produce. Subtract members and the limit is lower; add members and the limit is raised.

It is through the synergy of group members working together that a group is able to push through those limits. The word *synergy* became a buzz word during the 1980s. Groups were told to create synergy—produce more than the sum of their parts—but were not told how to do it. Facilitation is an important tool in helping groups and teams be

Table 5-4   Performing

Work to be done	Activities that will lead the group to accomplish its Charge and Charter.
	This often looks like: *producing the output expected of the group* (for example, fulfilling the Charge, described in Chapter 2).
Behaviors and dynamics that may be observed	• Clear role definition and ability to "flex" between roles • Collaboration • Interdependence • Experience of group strength • Achievement of consistent, excellent performance • Attainment of high group member satisfaction
Questions to be answered	• How will we know when we have been successful?
Problems that will continue to surface if not addressed	• Work not getting done • Group not knowing when it is falling short • Group not being able to celebrate its accomplishments

successful at this task. The key is utilizing interdependence within groups. In helping group members work together more effectively, facilitation promotes synergy. The Group Development Curve helps in understanding this connection.

Group Development Curve

Interdependence enables groups to break through the productivity limit and begin to achieve synergy. Facilitators have a major impact on its development. We have depicted the potential for group development and productivity improvement in the Group Development Curve in Figure 5-3 (page 72). This figure illustrates a number of stages in the development of groups.

Figure 5-3 **Group Development Curve**

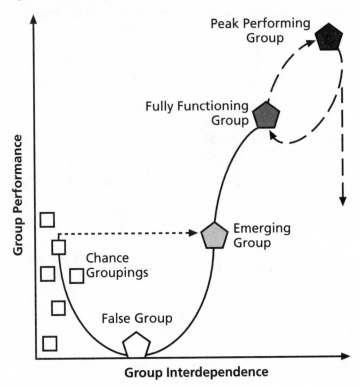

Descriptions of the stages

Groups that experience an expectation of *group performance* but little or no *group interdependence* are called **Chance Groupings**. They produce work through the efforts of individuals and do not create synergy. There is no expectation of significant interdependence among group members. Group members share information and coordinate tasks. Especially where personal relationships exist, members will help others complete their work.

Groups that experience a heightened level of *group interdependence* but little attention to *group performance* are called **False Groups**. Many False Groups have been unintentionally established in the rush to introduce teams into the workplace. Group members have little or no expectation about getting real work done, limiting their attention to how they interact. Others in their organization may notice they get little or nothing done and may belittle them by describing them as only "contemplating their navels." This has often been the outcome when companies have introduced "quality initiatives" into their organization. Group members were simply expected to know how to achieve the ill-defined results. Although they are often called teams or groups, they have not focused attention on their common purpose or the ways they work together. Without the necessary attention to the tasks to be done, the work produced by a False Group is less than the potential collective output of its individual members. If members of a False Group wish to progress on the Group Development Curve, they need to set their sights on the Emerging Group stage. They must become clear about the work they expect to do and how they intend to do it.

Groups that experience a heightened level of *group interdependence* and attend to *group performance* are called **Emerging Groups**. There is usually an expectation, both internal and external to the group, that members will work together to improve performance. These groups are often referred to as teams, but they need to pay additional attention to identifying their Charter. Creating the elements of a Charter produces substantial gains in group performance. The work produced by Emerging Groups matches or exceeds the output of Chance Groupings and has the potential for more. For Emerging Groups to continue their development, they must continue to refine their understanding of both the work to be done and ways they can work together more effectively. Effective facilitation produces much more rapid progress in moving to the next level.

As with False Groups, if participants in Chance Groupings decide to become more productive, they need to set their sights on becoming Emerging Groups. They do not have to follow the curve into the less productive area of False Groups. They can make the jump directly to Emerging Group by identifying their group Charge and then developing a group Charter. A facilitator can help accelerate this process.

Groups that experience significantly heightened levels of *group interdependence* and commitment to *group performance* are called **Fully Functioning Groups**. These groups have successfully attended to their group purpose, goals, roles, and procedures. They know what work needs to be done, how to do it, and when it is complete. The work produced by Fully Functioning Groups is of consistently high quality and quantity. These groups can sustain themselves over time, in the face of heavy demands. Becoming a Fully Functioning Group should be the objective for all groups. Fully Functioning Groups have a responsibility to maintain their position. It is a productive level that can be sustained. Fully Functioning Groups need to periodically review their Charge and Charter. A conscientious review process can help a Fully Functioning Group avoid falling into deep ruts. An effective facilitator helps Fully Functioning Groups maintain their productivity.

Fully Functioning Groups that experience a significant challenge or opportunity can temporarily lift their *group performance* and *group interdependence* to an even higher level. **Peak Performing Groups** are deeply committed to the achievement of the group's purpose and to each member's growth and success. The level of performance of Peak Performing Groups may surprise both group members and others. The synergy achieved can be truly amazing. Performance at this level is temporary because the energy and focus required are beyond what can be sustained by the group.

Some organizations expect all groups to be Peak Performing Groups, but this expectation often leads to burnout. The Peak Performing Group level must be temporary because of the exceptional energy and time required. Some Peak Performing Groups experience significant declines in productivity after meeting their major challenge. To avoid this, Peak Performing Groups should plan to return to the Fully Functioning Group level. They do this by celebrating, taking a little time off, or just resting for a short while. Effective facilitators help Peak Performing Groups both meet their challenge and successfully return to being a Fully Functioning Group.

Often when people look at the Group Development Curve they assume that the Peak Performing Group is the most desirable, but choosing to remain at this level is an error. The most desirable stage of group is the Fully Functioning Group, unless the situation does not require that level of performance. The least desired form of group is the False Group because it is very unproductive and may, at times, even drain productivity from other parts of the organization. Luckily, this form can be skipped by groups moving directly from Chance Groupings to Emerging Groups. Each group has the opportunity to decide which form or stage will work most effectively for its situation.

Facilitators can help groups both make those decisions and make progress toward their developmental goal. Table 5-5 summarizes both the choices groups face at each level of functioning and the tasks facilitators can be expected to complete.

Table 5-5 Group choices and facilitator tasks

Group Functioning	Group Choices	Facilitator Tasks
Chance Groupings	• Maintain as a Chance Grouping. • Improve productivity by becoming an Emerging Group.	• Very little facilitation activity required for Chance Grouping because there is little interdependence • Help group have more effective meetings • Help group consider whether it needs to be another type of group • Help group identify its Charge and develop its Charter if it wishes to change
False Groups	• Continue to meet without being productive. • Improve productivity by becoming an Emerging Group.	• Very little facilitation activity required for False Groups that wish to stay at that stage because there is little productivity or growth opportunity • Help group consider whether it needs to be another type of group • Help group identify its Charge and develop its Charter if it wishes to change
Emerging Groups	• Maintain level of productivity established by being an Emerging Group. • Progress toward becoming a Fully Functioning Group.	• Focus on and support the group adhering to its Charter • Help group consider whether it needs to be another type of group • Continue to both refine the processes used to be productive and encourage group interdependence

(continued on next page)

Table 5-5 Group choices and facilitator tasks (continued)

Group Functioning	Group Choices	Facilitator Tasks
Fully Functioning Groups	• Maintain level of productivity established by being a Fully Functioning Group. • Prepare to move to Peak Performing Group, as required.	• Focus on and support the group adhering to and periodically reviewing and revising its Charter • Assist group in being alert to demands that it function as a Peak Performing Group and develop plans for functioning at that level
Peak Performing Groups	• Ignore cost of being a Peak Performing Group and risk serious loss of productivity once challenge is over. • Prepare to return to being a Fully Functioning Group when challenge is over.	• Assist group in following its Charter to meet the particular challenge • Assist group to acknowledge it is performing beyond a self-sustaining level and to initiate its plan for effectively dealing with the situation

Observing group interactions

Observing provides the information that helps facilitators take the best action in any particular situation. Observing occurs at two levels. At the first level, facilitators simply watch particular exchanges among a group's members. They are then available and prepared to help if the exchange becomes unproductive. This level of observation requires the full presence and attention of the facilitator at that moment. Some exchanges can be so riveting that facilitators forget to intervene when they should. Not getting caught up in the drama of these exchanges is a skill that effective facilitators cultivate.

At the second level, facilitators must accumulate their first-level observations over time and then interpret them. This level requires reflection to detect patterns in the ways group members interact. Was a particular outburst from one group member an isolated incident or was it part of a pattern? What about the way the group worked easily to consensus when solving the latest problem? Why are several group members not talking to each other during group meetings?

The effective facilitator selectively shares these first- and second-level observations with the group in a process known as **reflection**. Using reflection appropriately is one of the most artistic aspects of facilitation. Different groups and different circumstances require different types of reflection. When reflecting observations to the group, the facilitator should begin by saying something like, "What I just heard was . . ." or "This is what I just saw happen." By using reflection, the facilitator helps the group pay attention to the way it works together. The group may not agree with the facilitator's observations or interpretations. The effective facilitator reflects in ways that allow the group members to respond and draw their own conclusions. Reflection is one of the strongest ways a facilitator can model helpful behavior.

Group relationship patterns

One of the patterns a facilitator will observe is the common ways group members relate to each other. These relationship patterns may range from adversarial to partnering. We have found it helpful to categorize these patterns to help facilitators both better understand their groups and decide what action they can take to help the groups be more productive. Figure 5-4 presents these categories on the adversarial-to-partnering continuum. Any of these forms of interaction can and will occur at times in every group. This is normal and natural.

What is important is which type of relationship is most common. Groups that demonstrate the more adversarial interactions are less able to work together effectively. They are likely to become stuck as a Chance Grouping, False Group, or Emerging Group. They find it harder to build the sense of interdependence that characterizes groups that progress to the Fully Functioning Group stage. They tend to look at specific solutions in terms of who succeeds and who fails: win–lose.

Figure 5-4   6C Relationship Model

Adversarial	Coercion	Confrontation	Coexistence	Cooperation	Collaboration	Co-Ownership	Partnering
	"You must do this or face pain."	"You must do this." "No, I won't!"	"You stay on your side and I'll stay on mine."	"I'll help you when my work is done."	"Let's work on this together."	"We both feel totally responsible."	

Win – Lose   Win – Win

The more partnering behavior at the right of the figure is typical of groups that are advancing in their development or maintaining as Fully Functioning Groups. The more they value partnering, the more often they look for solutions where everyone can be successful: win–win.

Each of these six forms of relationship has an impact both on the performance of a group and the satisfaction group members have in participating in it. Group members often do not use these labels to describe the ways they relate to each other, but they certainly recognize the behaviors associated with each type of interaction.

Coercion is all about the use of power to force a desired outcome. Coercion occurs when two group members have very different levels of power. A person's power may come from his or her position, personal character, or knowledge. People with power may be either very quiet or very loud in exercising their power, but it is clear who is being forced. Individuals who have both the managerial and facilitator roles must be careful not to use the manager's power to coerce while acting as a facilitator. Those who have less power may spend a lot of their resources protecting themselves. Those who have more power may spend resources maintaining their position. When coercion is the primary form of relationship, groups are unable to develop along the Group Development Curve. Any group synergy, or even interdependence, that tries to emerge is squashed by coercion.

Confrontation occurs between people who exercise more equal power. It is most noticeable when both choose to confront each other in a forceful, and often loud, way. Groups in which confrontation is common tend to focus more on these interactions than on the work itself. It is nearly impossible for a group to progress beyond Chance Grouping when confrontation is the primary form of relationship.

Coexistence may be equated to drawing a line in the sand, with parties agreeing not to cross into each other's territory. It is a clear statement that members are not interested in working with each other. Groups exhibiting coexistence do not experience the sense of common purpose necessary to work together. In fact, members actively work at not working together. It is hard for the group to look at the larger, groupwide, longer-range objectives because everyone is much more focused on completing his or her own assigned tasks.

Cooperation on this continuum continues to reflect a focus on individual tasks, but there are times when one person will help another complete his or her tasks. This occurs primarily when the helping people have some free time or are specifically asked to give assistance. In this environment, people do not volunteer readily to help out but can be responsive when asked. Group members still find it harder to identify with the group and with accomplishment of the group's Charge beyond how it impacts them directly.

Collaboration exists when group members identify with the group and seriously consider the group's overall Charge. Members experience a proportion of the responsibility for the success of the group; for example, if eight people are in the group, each feels one-eighth responsible. Groups in which this is the primary way members interact experience a significant sense of interdependence. This form of relationship is most common in Emerging Groups and Fully Functioning Groups.

Co-Ownership reflects a shift in group members' sense of responsibility. They now all feel 100% responsible for the success of the group. Individuals not only understand their roles and responsibilities, but they are willing to pitch in wherever they are needed to help the group be successful. They recognize their interdependence with others in the group and actively work to support them. This form of relationship is found most often in Fully Functioning and Peak Performing Groups.

The challenge for every facilitator is to help groups and teams progress to the point where they exhibit the types of relationships appropriate for the type of group they are seeking to be. For example, groups that wish to be Fully Functioning need to exhibit Collaborative and Co-Ownership behavior. Increasing the proportion of these behaviors within the group will help it progress along the Group

Figure 5-5   *TARGET Approach to Growth*

Truth

Accountability

Respect

Growth

Empowerment

Trust

Development Curve. To promote this growth, it is helpful to think of what contributes to working more in a partnering approach.

Trust is one of the most important characteristics of collaborative groups. A practical way for facilitators to help groups develop trust and to act more consistently on the partnering side of the continuum is to use the TARGET Approach to Growth, as illustrated in Figure 5-5. This is an easy-to-use method for identifying tangible areas in which facilitators can help groups to act in a more partnering way.

It is hard for group members to work in partnership with others when they do not know the **truth** (*T*) about expectations and experiences. By reflecting their own experiences back to groups, facilitators help create a climate where the truth can be told. Facilitators can model telling the truth and thereby positively reinforce group members, who also tell the truth. Withholding the truth "because certain group members couldn't handle it" or other similar reasons is not acceptable. Facilitators can take decisive action to call for the truth to be shared in groups.

The success of groups revolves around their being **accountable** (*A*). Group members agree to be accountable to each other for their work. Facilitators can structure opportunities for group members to clarify both their own tasks and what other group members expect of them. Facilitators can also ensure that there will be regular check-in points to review progress against the group's Charter.

It is difficult for group members to work in partnership with each other when they do not **respect** (R) each other. Respect in groups is most often based on members experiencing others as acting with integrity and being respectful themselves. For a facilitator, respect is a more challenging area to address because it tends to be so intangible. It is often closely tied to trust. When serious problems of insufficient respect arise within a group, a facilitator may need to name the problem directly and invite the group to develop a plan for addressing it. If members are really committed to being a Fully Functioning Group, they have to respect each other.

One of the key characteristics of a Fully Functioning Group is the commitment of individual group members and the group as a whole to **growth** (G). Growth in this context means increasing an individual's and a group's capability. By growing, the individual and group complete more difficult tasks, work more efficiently, and are recognized for their improvements. Facilitators can be helpful in this process by naming these changes as growth and helping both individuals and groups begin to value growing.

A critical change that takes place as groups move from the adversarial to partnering approach is the expectation that all group members will act increasingly on their own initiative to further the group's success. In coercive situations, people do as they are told, whereas in co-ownership situations they act independently, yet in concert. It is ironic that the most powerful partnering requires independent action. Partnering also requires group members to reflect their experience back to the group so the group can improve its processes. People acting in this way are being **empowered** (E) to act. They are expected to act in ways that help the group achieve success. Conversely, independent action is discouraged if the group or group leader disciplines an individual if his or her action turns out to be wrong. Such disciplining negatively reinforces the situation, leading to avoidance of the behavior that caused the problem: the independent action. Successful groups depend on independent action. Facilitators play an important role in helping groups identify where group members are expected to act independently yet in concert with the overall work of the group, as well as how they will reflect their experiences to the group.

Successfully building on each of these areas leads to **trust** (T) within a group. Members of Fully Functioning Groups trust each other. They know they can count on each other to complete their work or give the rest of the group sufficient opportunity to help. Trusting group members do not worry about covering up mistakes or what they can do to look good. They are concerned about working as effectively and efficiently as possible in close concert with everyone else in the group. Facilitators must be concerned with the level of trust in their groups. Although trust appears to be very intangible and often fragile, facilitators can help group members build their trust in one another and in the group. One of the most important ways they can do this is by helping groups identify where strong trust already exists and where trust is weakest. Discussions about trust are often difficult, and facilitators need to pay close attention to keep them productive. Successfully addressing the other areas of TARGET can also help because trust is built on these other areas.

Rank ordering of systems

Do I put my group ahead of my organization? If I work late frequently, am I saying my family is less important? One reason group dynamics is so complex is that we are all part of many systems. For example, an

Figure 5-6   Overlapping systems

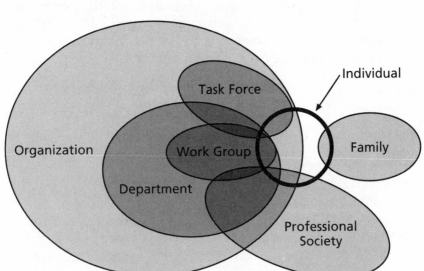

individual may be part of a work group, department, organization, and perhaps a professional association. He or she may also be part of a family. Each of these is a separate system. How do we feel about each of them? How important is the well-being of one system over the well-being of another?

Each of these systems has its unique impact on how an individual acts. The fulfillment of the needs of one system may compete with fulfilling the needs of another. The most obvious example here is the frequently competing needs of a person's family and organization. Each person deals with this situation by ranking the systems in their order of importance. This process is rarely discussed with others, and often the person is not even conscious of doing it.

Figure 5-6 illustrates how a typical person is part of a number of systems. In this example, the individual is part of several systems at work: the whole organization, the department, a work group, and a special task force. Participation in additional systems at work is possible: a group that eats together regularly, a company picnic planning committee, or a carpool. The individual is also part of a professional society, some of whose members work for the same organization and some who don't. In addition, the individual participates in a few of the professional society's activities outside the context of work. And, finally,

Figure 5-7 Rank ordering of overlapping systems

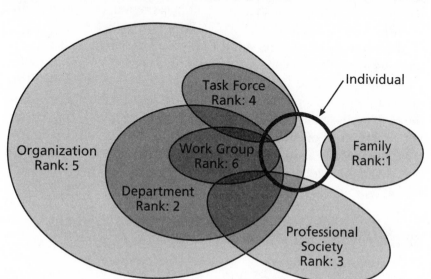

this individual is a member of a family. Other systems outside of work may also compete for the person's resources (time, energy, and so on): a church group, a social circle, bowling or racquetball team, theater troop, or musical group. The individual may also have another job.

These systems do not operate in isolation. The competing demands, expectations, and standards of each system have to be considered. Doing so would be a tremendous amount of work if all the systems were equal, but people avoid the problem by ranking them. The higher a system is ranked, the more thoroughly it is considered. Other, less significant systems are relegated to the periphery, where they receive cursory consideration at best. Figure 5-7 (page 83) describes how an individual might rank the systems presented in the earlier example.

Facilitators face a real challenge in dealing with groups where each group member is rank ordering his or her systems differently. The more the needs of different systems are in competition, the fewer resources the lower-ranked system will receive. The higher-ranked systems will use as many of the resources as necessary to fulfill their needs. What is left over is used in lower-ranked systems. Because the needs of these systems vary, the resources available to the lower-ranked systems vary as well. This can mean the resources group members can contribute to a group may be very different from one point in time to another. One example of this would be a crisis with the family—a sick child or a death in the family—which may very well mean the person does not even come in to work. Another example would be an approaching project deadline, when group members put in extra hours to complete the project on time.

Facilitators who understand that group members will be rank ordering their systems can create opportunities for their groups to talk about their priorities more openly. Groups can then recognize that unless there has been agreement on these priorities, the differences in the rankings is fertile ground for misunderstanding. Many group member expectations of themselves and others are based on these rankings. Discussions about how the various systems are ranked can be a useful tool for helping groups work together more effectively.

Working with group dynamics

Although facilitators need not be experts in group dynamics to help groups get their work done, the best facilitators are students of how group members work together. They seek to better understand how group members interact, and they pay careful attention to the groups they facilitate.

The first step facilitators can take to work effectively with group dynamics is to understand a group's history. Groups do not operate in isolation. Behaviors exhibited in groups can be understood in terms of what has happened before within the group, within other groups, and what is happening in the larger organization. The 'Orming Model is helpful in understanding the behaviors resulting from the movement of people in and out of the group as well as from major changes in the group's Charge. Facilitators can help groups do the work necessary in the Forming, Storming, Norming, and Performing stages. Groups who accept as normal, behaviors associated with these stages do not interpret them as setbacks. This is a more helpful perspective.

To be in a position to optimally complete their tasks, different groups need to operate at different positions on the Group Development Curve. Some groups may be very successful as Chance Groupings. They do not need the advantages gained from higher group interdependence, and they can avoid the investment of time and creativity necessary to build effective group interdependence. Other groups absolutely require the synergy that is possible in Fully Functioning or Peak Performing Groups. For them, the investment of resources pays important dividends. Furthermore, recognizing a group as a False Group is a red flag for facilitators. This is a group that needs to move elsewhere on the curve if it is to be productive.

The relationship patterns within groups either help or hinder these groups in being successful. Groups that operate in a more Coercive, Confrontational, or Coexistence manner are not effective in creating the synergy that creates breakthrough levels of productivity. This behavior is more common in Chance Groupings or even Emerging Groups. Cooperative, Collaborative, or Co-Ownership behaviors are necessary for groups to reach the Fully Functioning and Peak Performing Group stages. Facilitators must take specific action to help groups work together more effectively. This can be especially challenging when conflict arises. Chapter 6 presents an approach that will help groups discover how conflict is an important asset.

CHAPTER 6

Dealing with Conflict

In this chapter you will learn:

- Conflict Response Modes
- Victim-Persecutor-Rescuer Triangle
- Conflict Resolution Steps

*E*very group experiences conflict. The challenge is how to handle it more effectively. Conflict is most often experienced as an open, often verbally and/or possibly physically violent, clash between individuals or groups. Some people find these open clashes to be exciting, whereas others seek to avoid them. People tend to take conflict very personally. Facilitators need to be aware that conflict occurs in groups in many more forms than just the open, often emotional, clashes between people.

Groups struggle with conflict because they lack experience in dealing with it effectively. Individuals and groups often work with the assumption that conflict is "bad." Many believe that open expression of conflict is a sign of a poorly performing group. Thus, people will sometimes avoid conflict. A facilitator does a group a disservice when he or she tries to push the group through conflict too quickly, or avoid it altogether.

A good place to start understanding conflict is looking at its definition. We define conflict simply as *unresolved differences*. In group settings, dealing with conflict means resolving differences in ways that help the group get its work done and function together more effectively. By focusing on task, facilitators help groups experience conflict as differences of ideas or opinions rather than as personal battles where there will be winners and losers. Some group members will prefer to express their differences in a loud, intimidating style; others will choose a quieter, more reserved approach. Facilitators need to support both styles to help groups resolve their differences in productive ways.

Facilitators can help groups see conflict in new ways by asking them the following questions:

1. What is it like when nobody disagrees?
2. How is synergy created when nobody disagrees?

The resulting dialogue enables groups to explore the positive aspects of conflict. *Conflict is a healthy sign that individuals in the group care about the quality of their work and wish to find solutions to their problems.* Conflict can become a serious problem in groups that have no process for dealing with it effectively.

Fully Functioning and Peak Performing Groups *depend on conflict* to create the synergy they desire. They do not promote divisive forms of conflict but seek to draw out the differences within the group. These groups know that they need the differences in order to create the desired synergy. They have found groups with no disagreements to be boring and less productive because working in these groups adds nothing to solving problems. Fully Functioning and Peak Performing Groups know the purpose of conflict in their group setting: the full expression of differences. They also know how to resolve the conflicts and move on. One important job of the facilitator is to help the group understand that conflicts that do arise can contribute to the success of the group. The facilitator can introduce tools and processes that help the group work through conflict to produce a positive result.

Conflict Response Modes

Ralph Kilmann and Kenneth Thomas developed a pioneering model for better understanding individuals' preferences for dealing with conflict situations. "Conflict situations" are situations where people appear to have different desires, needs, wants, opinions, or beliefs. Thomas and Kilmann described a person's behavior along two basic dimensions: (1) *assertiveness*, the extent to which the individual

Figure 6-1 Conflict Modes

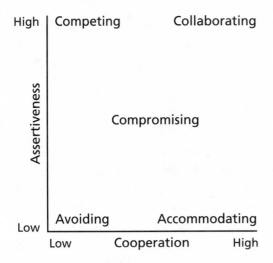

attempts to satisfy his or her own concerns, and (2) *cooperativeness*, the extent to which the individual attempts to satisfy the other person's concerns. These two basic dimensions of behavior can be used to define five specific methods of dealing with conflicts. These five "conflict-handling modes" are shown in Figure 6-1.

These modes are well known in our culture. Conventional wisdom recognizes, for example, that often "Two heads are better than one" (Collaborating). But it also says: "Kill your enemies with kindness" (Accommodating), "Split the difference" (Compromising), "Leave well enough alone" (Avoiding), and "Might makes right" (Competing). The effectiveness of a specific conflict-handling mode depends on the requirements of the situation and the skill with which the mode is used.

What the Modes mean

Building on the work of Thomas and Kilmann, we have developed additional descriptive materials for these five modes. Our approach recognizes that everyone is capable of operating from any of the modes but that everyone prefers one or more styles over others. Preferences for dealing with conflict may also vary in different types of environments (for example, work or home) for a particular individual. Usually, this preference is exercised without an individual making a conscious choice. It is automatic. When our preferred mode does not seem to work, we shift to another.

There is no inherently "good" or "bad" mode. For each mode, there are situations where its use can be the most productive. Conversely, there are situations where its use is quite counterproductive. Individuals who are aware of the choices and of their own preferences can determine which will be the most effective mode in a particular situation. They can also assess how skilled they are at using each of the modes and practice the ones they are less comfortable with. The end result is an increased flexibility in dealing with conflict.

The owner of a large restaurant and delicatessen was struggling to deal with a conflict between his two kitchen managers. Both managers were responsible for scheduling staff, supervising production and cleanup, and developing new menu items. One manager preferred to develop new menu items, sometimes letting the other duties go undone. Because many of this manager's new items had increased sales at the deli, the owner asked the other kitchen manager to pick up the slack. This was met with accusations of favoritism and a threat to quit.

The owner tried facilitating a meeting of the three, but it quickly erupted when the dissatisfied kitchen manager started yelling loudly. The owner and the other manager sat in stunned silence. The owner let the manager vent his feelings until he began to quiet down. When calm returned, the upset kitchen manager appeared to be somewhat embarrassed by his outburst. The owner began to explore what it was about the change that was so disturbing to the manager. And the manager responded: He had never been recognized for his success in keeping the kitchen running smoothly. He found the sudden recognition of the other manager for creating new menu items to be offensive. The three were able to discover a solution that was fully acceptable to both kitchen managers. The result was improved operation of the kitchen and an increased flow of exciting new menu items.

Facilitators can benefit from both knowing their own preferences and recognizing the preferences of group members. Having this flexibility to make conscious choices in how to deal with particular conflicts gives a facilitator a powerful tool for interacting with groups. Helping group members learn about and use the modes not only improves their ability to deal with conflict but also expands their language for communicating about their interactions.

Avoiding is unassertive and uncooperative. The individual does not immediately pursue his or her own concerns or those of the other person. He or she does not address conflict. Avoiding might take the form of diplomatically sidestepping an issue, postponing an issue until a better time, or simply withdrawing from a threatening situation.

Competing is assertive and uncooperative. An individual pursues her or his own concerns at the other person's expense. This is a power-oriented mode in which one uses whatever power seems appropriate (for example, one's ability to argue, one's rank, or economic sanctions) to win one's own position. Competing might mean "standing up for your rights," defending a position you believe is correct, or simply trying to win.

Accommodating is unassertive and cooperative. When Accommodating, an individual neglects his or her own concerns to satisfy the concerns of the other person; there is an element of self-sacrifice in this mode. Accommodating might take the form of selfless generosity or charity, obeying another person's order when one would prefer not to, or yielding to another's point of view.

Collaborating is both assertive and cooperative. Collaborating involves an attempt to work with the other person to find some solution that fully satisfies the concerns of both persons. It means digging into an issue to identify the underlying concerns of the two individuals in order to find an alternative that meets both sets of concerns. Collaboration between two people might take the form of exploring a disagreement to learn from the insights of each, committing to resolve some condition that would otherwise have the two competing for resources, or confronting and trying to find a creative solution to an interpersonal problem.

Compromising is intermediate in both assertiveness and cooperativeness. The objective here is to find some quick, mutually acceptable solution that partially satisfies both parties. It falls on a middle ground between Competing and Accommodating. Compromising gives up more than Competing but less than Accommodating. Likewise, it addresses an issue more directly than Avoiding, but does not explore it in as much depth as Collaborating. Compromising might mean splitting the difference, exchanging concessions, or seeking a quick middle-ground position.

Using the Modes

Each person is capable of employing any of the five conflict-handling modes. No one can be characterized as having a single, rigid style of dealing with conflict. However, any given individual is more comfortable with certain modes, using them more often and effectively, and, therefore, tending to rely on them more heavily than on others. This preference is often related to a person's temperament and experience.

The conflict-handling behaviors an individual uses are, therefore, a result of both personal predispositions and the requirements of specific situations. Tables 6-1 through 6-5 each focus on a particular style, presenting situations for which the use of that style is appropriate and giving examples of both group members and facilitators using that Conflict Mode.

Table 6-1 Avoiding: Do not address the situation at this time

Uses	Group Member Example	Facilitator Example
• When an issue is less important than others • When you perceive no chance of satisfying your concerns, or the issue seems off the track or symptomatic of another, more basic issue • When the potential damage of confronting a conflict outweighs the benefits of its resolution • To let people cool down; to reduce tension as well as to regain perspective and composure • To let others resolve the conflict more effectively • When gathering more information outweighs the advantages of an immediate solution	One group member listens to a discussion between two others who are upset about a particular company policy. They are in the office of one of the two upset group members. The first group member agrees with the policy, but she remains quiet, and the conversation soon turns back to topics of a higher concern to her.	A facilitator is concerned with the behavior of a couple of group members. Contrary to their usual behavior, they are acting in a manner disruptive to the group process. The facilitator is unsure why they are acting in this way and decides to wait a while before intervening. Over the next few minutes, the disruptive group members share information that helps the facilitator understand what is happening. The facilitator did not need to take any action.

Table 6-2   Competing: Focus on your perspective, regardless of others

Uses	Group Member Example	Facilitator Example
• When quick, decisive action is vital (e.g., in emergencies) • On important issues where unpopular courses of action need implementation (e.g., supporting unpopular rules, insisting on a particular course of action) • On issues vital to group welfare when you know you are right • To protect yourself against people who take advantage of noncompetitive behavior	A group member has had experience with the problem currently facing the group. Although they have never faced this situation before, several other members are assertively advocating that the group take action the first group member is certain will not work. The first group member takes a very strong stand in opposition to the proposed action.	The facilitator has watched two group members continue to make negative comments about each other, and it is beginning to disrupt the process of the group. The facilitator takes a stand that the behavior has to end if the group is to be successful. The two group members agree and the group gets back to work.

Victim-Rescuer-Persecutor Triangle

Conflict situations tend to become much more intense when at least one person operates from the Competing mode. In groups experienced in dealing with conflict, this intensity adds to the energy available to the group. In less experienced groups, however, these situations can become explosive. They also may cause group members to play one of the three positions often associated with intense conflict: **victim**, **rescuer**, or **persecutor**.   These positions have been learned in families, social settings, and work environments. The persecutor harasses or oppresses a victim. The victim is in obvious pain, and someone tries to rescue the victim from the persecutor. Often, to the surprise of the rescuer, both the victim and persecutor turn on the rescuer. The rescuer becomes the victim as the positions shift. An example of this would

Table 6-3 *Accommodating: Focus on other's perspective, regardless of your own*

Uses	Group Member Example	Facilitator Example
• When you realize you are wrong, to allow a better position to be heard, to learn from others, and to show that you are reasonable • When the issue is much more important to the other person than to you, to satisfy the needs of others, and as a goodwill gesture to help maintain a cooperative relationship • To create an obligation on the other's part to support you on issues that are more important to you • When preserving harmony and avoiding disruption are especially important • To aid in the development of group members by allowing them to experiment and learn from their own mistakes	A group member who always has an idea for how to do everything has just made a suggestion. Another group member, who usually is very quiet, speaks up in a trembling voice, proposing an alternative approach. He adds a few comments that make it clear that using this approach is very important to him. The first group member decides to back off from her idea and support the contribution of the usually quieter member.	The facilitator is talking with one of her group members, using this opportunity to gain feedback on the series of steps she has designed for the group to follow to evaluate particular information and make a decision. The group member strongly objects to the proposed steps. Although the facilitator is certain that the steps are the best way to proceed, she agrees to the alternative proposed by the group member. She hopes the process will work all right and the group will support the outcome more if she does not get into a struggle about which steps to use.

Table 6-4 Collaborating: All members get what they want, maybe more

Uses	Group Member Example	Facilitator Example
• To find an integrative solution when both sets of concerns are too important to be compromised • When your objective is to learn (e.g., testing your own assumptions, understandings of others) • To blend insights from people with different perspectives • To gain commitment by incorporating others' concerns into a consensus decision • To work through hard feelings, which have been interfering with an interpersonal relationship	Several group members have taken what, at first, appear to be strong mutually exclusive positions. They all say their position is very important to them and they don't want to compromise. One of the group members, who had been quiet until now, speaks up. He feels the final solution needs to take both positions into account and the group should take the time to create it. The group's discussion then changes from a focus on the particulars of the disagreement to a focus on the symbolism or impact of the differences (e.g., meeting a suggested intermediate deadline symbolizes how capable a group is or that the whole project is on track to be completed on time). Once the group focuses on the essence of the desired solution, it is able to identify a win–win solution.	A facilitator is concerned with group members who are not working together very well. The members have intense feelings about the topic at hand and are getting very stuck. The facilitator interrupts the discussion to make process observations and strongly suggests the group take a few moments to improve the process. Several group members do not want to leave the topic on the table. Exploring the essence of what the group members and facilitator want reveals that both want to improve the group process, get unstuck, and gain group agreement on the discussion topic. Together, they are able to identify a way of using the topic to improve their process and also progress toward the desired resolution.

Table 6-5   *Compromising: Everyone gives a little*

Uses	Group Member Example	Facilitator Example
• When goals are moderately important but not worth the effort or potential disruption of more assertive modes • When two opponents with equal power are strongly committed to perceived mutually exclusive goals (e.g., labor–management bargaining) • To achieve temporary settlements to complex issues • To arrive at quick solutions under time pressures • As a backup mode when Collaboration or Competition fails	Two group members have taken strongly opposing stands. After they have presented their positions for a period of time, one of them suggests there might be some middle ground. The other agrees to a proposed compromise. The negotiation moves quickly and soon the group is able to move on.	A facilitator has been observing the interactions of her group and is concerned that many of them are hurting the group's performance. She shares her concerns with the group, and they embark on a lengthy discussion. The facilitator presents a set of steps to resolve the problems. Several group members express their desire to take less time on this issue, due to their heavy workloads. The group and facilitator agree to spend 15 minutes discussing her observations and then follow up in two weeks.

be one group member verbally attacking (persecuting) another group member (victim). A third group member gets tired of the attack and jumps in to protect (rescue) the individual receiving the attack. To the surprise of the rescuer, the victim reacts angrily and attacks (now persecuting) the rescuer (now a victim) for meddling. This third person is offended because the intent was only to try to help, and he or she then strikes back verbally (persecutes). This fluid dynamic is described in Figure 6-2.

Facilitators are vulnerable to getting caught up in this triangle. They see a situation and intervene to help the group operate more effectively. To their surprise, they are suddenly put on the defensive

Figure 6-2 *Victim-Rescuer-Persecutor Triangle*

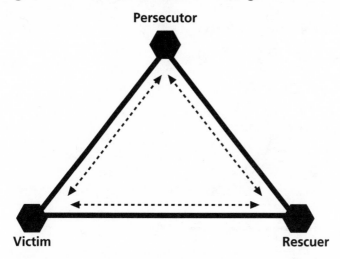

when they were only trying to help. The facilitator might get angry about this turn of events and switch positions once more to become the persecutor. Group members, group leaders, and facilitators are all prone to jump into these positions, usually without thinking. However, assuming these positions is not helpful in resolving conflict situations.

To be productive in intense conflict situations, facilitators must be aware of the seductive powers of these positions and make a different choice. The positions in the triangle personalize the conflict. When people are stuck in this triangle, they take everything very much to heart. Objectivity and a larger view are impossible to maintain. Facilitators and group members can learn to consciously choose not to enter these positions or, once in them, recognize what has happened and step back out. Figure 6-3 (page 98) depicts this neutral position on a different plane, above the triangle. Taking this different position provides a perspective that enables the observer/participant to continue being involved in the situation without getting caught up in the positions found in the triangle.

The obvious challenge in this situation is how to control your emotions in the heat of an exchange so that the neutral position can be attained. If a person is angry, afraid, or hurt, the most common response is to lash out at whomever he or she perceives caused the anger or hurt. *The urge to get even is strong.* This dynamic describes the experience of bouncing back and forth between being a victim and being a persecutor.

Figure 6-3 Taking the neutral position

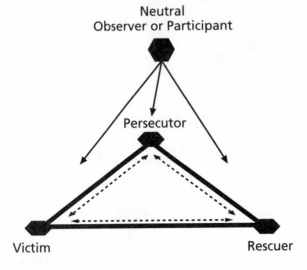

Emotions *do not have to be put on hold.* A clear expression of your experience, including your emotional response, fits with the neutral position. This clear expression of your experience can lead to collective problem solving, whereas using your emotions as a weapon pushes people further apart.

It is important that facilitators strive to position themselves in this neutral perspective so they can help group members step out of the Victim-Persecutor-Rescuer Triangle and operate more effectively. Facilitators do this by consciously choosing not to take the conflict personally. This choice is different from sitting on the sidelines vowing to just watch. Facilitators can implement this choice best by focusing on the ways people are interacting, rather than on the content of what people are saying. Remember, much of the important information is being shared nonverbally. Taking this position can be especially difficult for a facilitator who is also a manager who is responsible for the outcome. Gathering information and then helping the group move into the Conflict Resolution Steps can be the most effective way to create the best outcome.

Conflict Resolution Process

Resolving conflict means that the issue is considered closed by the person concerned about it. Resolution means that the person will not engage in the conflict (Avoiding), will gain his or her own solution (Competing), will agree to the other person's solution (Accommodating), will create a win–win solution (Collaborating), or will agree to a middle ground (Compromising). Achieving a Collaboration or Compromise solution does not happen by "magic." It happens because people care enough and know how to work through a resolution process.

There are five steps in the Conflict Resolution Process: expression of differences, awareness of conflict, clarification of differences, agreement of commonality, and resolution of conflict. In Table 6-6, we describe what to do to complete the steps and the impact on each step of the particular Conflict Mode chosen. All five steps will be completed only if either Collaboration or Compromise is chosen. Choosing other modes requires fewer steps.

The first step in the cycle is an **expression of differences**. This is when the differences are first given voice. In most situations, the differences will be in the form of statements and/or questions between

Table 6-6 *Conflict Resolution Process*

Steps	Situation	Impact of Mode Chosen
Step One: Expression of Differences Facilitators observe the verbal and nonverbal communication.	Whether calmly or emotionally expressed, this is the first indication that there are differences; only one side of the difference may be expressed at this point. If the conflict returns to this stage, differences are expressed without opportunity for a Collaborative outcome. Conflict will either continue indefinitely or end due to one side winning.	This step occurs for all modes chosen.

(continued on next page)

Table 6-6   *Conflict Resolution Process (continued)*

Steps	Situation	Impact of Mode Chosen
Step Two: Awareness of Conflict Facilitators can identify the conflict situation to the group and give the group an opportunity to use the rest of the Conflict Resolution Steps.	The differences are noted by at least one party of the conflict; this awareness may or may not be communicated to the other party. If the differences are openly discussed, agreement can be made to create a satisfactory resolution. If a conflict has recycled back to expression of differences, the parties can choose another conflict style at any time and either end the conflict or proceed to the next step: agreement on commonality.	This step triggers either an automatic or conscious selection of a Conflict Mode. If Avoidance is chosen, the conflict process stops at this point because only the other party is invested in a particular outcome; the parties may agree to disagree so everyone can get on with his or her work. If Accommodation is chosen, the conflict process stops at this point because one party acquiesces to the other. If Competition is chosen, the conflict returns to expression of differences. If Compromise or Collaboration is chosen, the parties proceed to agreement on commonality.

(continued on next page)

Table 6-6 *Conflict Resolution Process (continued)*

Steps	Situation	Impact of Mode Chosen
Step Three: Clarification of Differences Facilitators help the group gather information about either the bargaining points or the essences of what they need for a win–win solution.	Each party has the opportunity to explain his or her position and respond to clarifying questions by the other.	Using Compromise, the focus of the exchange is in identifying bargaining points—what can be given up to gain in other areas; this process usually takes less time. Using Collaboration, the focus of the exchange is on identifying the essence of each party's position—what each party needs to gain to win in a win–win outcome; this process usually takes more time.
Step Four: Agreement on Commonality Facilitators assist the group to identify points at which they are in agreement.	Parties to the conflict identify the benefits of achieving a mutually agreeable resolution. For example, although people feel strongly about the differences, everyone is committed to the group fulfilling its Charge and therefore wants to resolve the conflict.	Compromise and Collaboration take time and energy. The agreement on commonality provides the rationale for expending the time and energy.

(continued on next page)

Table 6-6   Conflict Resolution Process (continued)

Steps	Situation	Impact of Mode Chosen
Step Five: Resolution of Conflict Facilitators keep the discussion focused on reaching agreement and help the group recognize when it has achieved agreement.	Both parties identify and commit to a solution that satisfactorily resolves the conflict.	Using Compromise, each side gives up something in order to gain in other areas. Using Collaboration, each side is able to gain the essential elements that were sought.

two or more people. In some cases, the questions or statements will be in the form of thoughts in the minds of one or more group members (for example, one person, without stating it out loud, thinks of a position contrary to the one already presented to the group). Whether or not the differences are expressed to others, the differences trigger an awareness in someone that there is a conflict.

The second step in this process is **awareness of conflict**. This is an important step because it causes each person to initiate one of the five Conflict Modes. If either Avoidance or Accommodation is chosen, the individual does not pursue the conflict further. If Competing is chosen, this individual tries to jump two steps and impose a resolution. If Collaborating or Compromising is chosen, the next step is **clarification of differences**. Which Conflict Mode is used has a big impact on this step. Those using the Compromising mode seek information to determine the most successful bargaining strategy. Those using Collaboration seek to understand the essence of the outcome that the other wants.

The best resolutions to conflict come from situations where both the differences and the points of agreement are openly discussed. **Agreement of commonality** provides reasons for continuing the work of finding a resolution. People do not pursue collaborative or compromise resolutions of particular conflicts when they do not experience building on some form of existing agreement. Whether it is "By resolving this conflict well, we can create an even better solution" or "We have to resolve this or we can't finish this project," this agreement is necessary. Often, when there is a disagreement, people jump to the conclusion that they disagree about everything or nearly everything about the subject. However, usually they agree upon more than they realize.

It is out of the clarification of differences that individuals and groups come to better understand the particulars of the disagreement. The challenge is for people to communicate their perspectives and differences, as well as listen to the perspectives of others. Often, one person does not feel heard by the others and simply raises the volume of the discussion. The Conflict Resolution Process requires both parties to present their positions as clearly as possible and listen to other's positions.

It is amazing how a clear agreement of commonality and a productive clarification of differences creates a **resolution**. Resolution builds on the commonality, using the differences as ways to enrich the final solution. This is where synergy is really created. This is where groups can experience the outcome of conflict as a very positive part of its very existence.

Facilitators can use the following questions to help their groups work through the Conflict Resolution Process:

1. What is the issue or problem?
   How the issue or problem is stated often determines the outcome.
2. Where do we not agree?
   Areas of disagreement must be identified so they can be dealt with as separate issues or problems to be resolved.
3. Where (as we discuss the issue) can we agree?
   Areas of agreement are identified as a way of establishing a good foundation for the eventual solution.
4. Can we develop options that take advantage of the areas where we agree, and bring us closer in the areas where we disagree?
   Options are developed to take advantage of the areas of disagreement.

5. What action(s) will we take as next steps that will resolve the conflict?

    Actions represent what each party will do as a result of the discussion: What by Whom by When.

Capitalizing on conflict

Groups need to experience and resolve conflicts in order to be successful. The challenge is to use the conflict in productive rather than destructive ways. Many groups perceive conflict as something "bad." They feel it should either be avoided or it will be painful and disrupt the smooth working of the group. However, groups that do not experience conflict are less interesting, less productive groups. Responding to conflict in effective ways becomes a major asset for groups. Facilitators can help groups resolve conflict successfully when they listen well to their groups. Listening is the subject of Chapter 8.

CHAPTER 7

The Process of Effective Facilitation

In this chapter you will learn:

- The Process element of the Facilitation Model
- The three fundamental work processes and how they are useful to facilitators
- How to plan and facilitate effective meetings
- Nine tools facilitators use most often to help groups complete their work

*P*rocess is the fourth element of the Facilitation Model. We define Process as *what a facilitator does to help a group get its work done.* This is where the facilitator draws on what he or she has learned about Self and Group to help groups accomplish their tasks. Because they are aware of and understand the dynamics of their groups, effective facilitators ask timely, probing questions and make insightful observations. They are in a position to offer guidance if their groups go off-track, providing structure to discussions to help groups refocus on their tasks. These facilitators are also skilled at using a variety of tools (brainstorming, consensus, process mapping, and so on) to help groups do their work.

Facilitators' three fundamental processes

In their efforts to help groups complete tasks, facilitators use three fundamental processes that align with the natural progression of a group's work: (1) planning, (2) solving problems, and (3) finishing work.

A group that is planning is determining how it will complete a task. A planning activity is one that looks to the future. A group involved in problem solving focuses on what obstacles might be challenging it and what options are available. A problem-solving activity is one that looks to the present. A group that is finishing its work declares its task to be complete. The group looks at the work it has done, and is able to turn its attention to new tasks.

These fundamental processes look familiar to most people with managerial experience. What is different is *the way these processes are used*. Managers hoping to get the most from their groups *facilitate* these fundamental processes. They do not dictate project plans or provide problem solutions to their groups.

How are these three fundamental processes useful to managers attempting to use the role of facilitator? When determining what work a group is doing, or needs to do, a facilitator asks, "What is the group trying to accomplish at this moment?" The answer to that question leads the facilitator to the particular fundamental work process that needs attention.

How to tell which fundamental process is coming into play

When a group is planning, it discusses such things as: (1) how work will get done, (2) what resources will be available, (3) what constraints will be placed on the group, and/or (4) what success will look like. For groups trying to plan, facilitators ask questions to help the group focus on the future and articulate what it is trying to accomplish.

When a group is solving problems, it discusses such things as: (1) what obstacles are preventing it from getting the work done, (2) what options are available, (3) what criteria should be used to make decisions, and (4) how should decisions be made. For groups trying to solve a problem, facilitators ask questions to help the group focus on the present and describe what is happening at that moment.

When a group is finishing its work, facilitators will observe group members: (1) celebrating success, (2) expressing disappointment about an activity that failed, (3) talking excitedly about achieving a project milestone, and/or (4) turning attention to other matters. For groups in the process of finishing work, facilitators ask questions to help them determine if they have accomplished their goals.

Table 7-1 describes facilitators' three fundamental processes, giving specific examples of group activities and the actions facilitators take to help.

Table 7-1 *Examples of facilitator actions using the three fundamental processes*

Group Activities	Facilitator Actions	Tools That Can Be Used
P L A N N I N G Prepare an annual budget	Help the group come to consensus on its expense limits.	• Affinity diagram • Brainstorming • Cause-effect diagram • Consensus • Debrief • Force field analysis • Multi-voting • Parking lot • Process mapping
Set a meeting agenda	Ask clarifying questions about the purpose of the meeting.	
Draft a purpose statement for a Charter	Help the group brainstorm action verbs that describe what it does every day.	
S O L V I N G Resolve a conflict about a deadline	Ask group members how meeting the deadline will help them fulfill their Charge.	• Affinity diagram • Brainstorming • Cause-effect diagram • Consensus • Debrief • Force field analysis • Multi-voting • Parking lot • Process mapping
P R O B L E M S Make decisions about research project funding	Help the group brainstorm criteria for making its decision.	
Troubleshoot a new software product	Help the group complete a cause-effect diagram.	
Improve the efficiency of a packaging line	Help the group complete a process map and brainstorm ways to eliminate waste.	

(continued on next page)

Table 7-1   Examples of facilitator actions using the three fundamental processes *(continued)*

Group Activities	Facilitator Actions	Tools That Can Be Used
F I N I S H I N G W O R K Say good-bye to a group member	Facilitate a meeting to discuss how the group member has contributed to completing the Charter.	• Consensus • Debrief
Turn in an annual budget for final approval	Ask the group to debrief their budgeting process. Ask members if they have consensus that the budget really is final. Encourage them to think of ways to improve the process, making notes for next year.	
Celebrate the successful completion of a sales campaign	Encourage them to celebrate! And remember—let the group be the star!	

Planning

To successfully complete their tasks, groups need to be able to make plans quickly and follow them. Many groups have had bad experiences when they tried to plan. A common complaint is that "we spend too much time planning and not enough time doing." Effective facilitators help groups experience their planning as a valuable investment. How do they do this? Facilitators provide tools to help groups plan efficiently. They push groups to be rigorous so their plans produce the results the groups want. To help groups plan effectively, facilitators ask the following questions:

1. What are you trying to accomplish? What is your goal?

2. Is the goal realistic? Who should be accountable for its completion?
3. How does this goal support completing the group's Charter?
4. What will it look like when the goal is successfully completed?
5. What specific steps are needed to accomplish the goal? What do you need to do?

A group's Charter is an example of a plan

The Charter, which consists of a group's purpose, goals, roles, and procedures, is really a special type of plan. It helps a group be clear about both its overall task and how its members will work together. During the life of a typical group, the Charter is one of the larger-scale plans it produces. A group may draft a Charter only once, and update it only when group members come and go or when their Charge changes.

Every goal from a group Charter requires the group to create one or more project plans. A project plan thus can be thought of as a scaled-down Charter. Just like the group Charter, a project plan contains a purpose (sometimes called an objective) and one or more goals (sometimes called milestones). To accomplish the goals and fulfill the project purpose, groups devise a series of steps to follow. Facilitators help groups plan projects by asking questions that assist the group to clarify the purpose of the project.

When setting goals or milestones for the project, facilitators push a group to use the "What by Whom by When" format, just as the group did when setting the goals in the Charter. With practice, groups will automatically answer these three questions when defining their action steps: (1) What will we do? (2) Who is accountable for doing it? (3) When will it be done? Setting action steps in this format contributes to good planning and makes it easier for group members to follow through.

Every project and task has its own challenges. Good planning helps groups prepare for and meet these challenges. Facilitators help groups make plans efficiently so they can solve problems and finish their work.

A manager was preparing to facilitate his organization's annual business planning retreat. The group was skilled in the planning process and was interested in both improving the quality of the plan and reducing the time needed to complete the plan from four days to two. The manager told the group, "This will be possible if you work with me to design the retreat agenda."

The group designed a flexible agenda. Then they introduced some new technology and methods to speed up the process. One group member suggested using a laptop computer with an LCD projection screen to create the final business plan document during the retreat. Group members agreed to rotate responsibility for entering data throughout the two-day retreat.

During the first day of the retreat, the manager used a somewhat directive facilitation style because the group asked him to. At the end of the day, the group was slightly behind schedule and felt that finishing the plan by the end of the next day was at risk. The manager asked the group, "What went well today, and what could have gone better?" From the answers to this question, the group made adjustments in the agenda for the second day. They decided to use a simpler, less time-consuming decision-making process. The group completed the business plan by the end of the retreat. One group member told the manager, "We get better at this every year, and facilitation has made the biggest difference. And not just because you are the facilitator, but because we all know how to facilitate." The manager agreed.

Solving problems

Groups encounter problems every day. Questions, situations, and people present difficult, perplexing problems that groups have to solve if they are to be successful. Facilitators help groups systematically solve problems, using the following approach:

1. Accurately describe the problem itself.
2. Gather information—both qualitative and quantitative data.
3. Determine the most important factors contributing to the problem.
4. Describe what would be happening if things were going well.
5. Create action steps to solve the problem.

Combining these first four steps is essentially a "gap analysis," which is describing the difference between the current situation and the potentially ideal situation. The following are questions a facilitator asks a group to help it work through the gap analysis on its way to taking action to solve problems:

1. What is happening now?
2. What measures or other information do we have that tells us about what is happening now?
3. What is contributing to the problem?
4. What would be happening if things were going well?
5. What do we need to do to solve this problem? What specific actions do we need to take?

Gap analysis probably looks familiar to experienced managers. Traditional managers perform gap analyses themselves, and then assign others to close the gap they have identified. Managers who use the facilitator role to help groups complete gap analyses get more commitment for action because group members have helped define the problem and identify potential solutions.

Groups tend to jump to solutions too quickly

One of the biggest challenges groups face is the temptation to produce instant solutions. With pressure on organizations growing, we see this happen all too frequently. What can facilitators do to help groups cope with this pressure and solve problems successfully? Position the problem-solving process as a time-saver. Using the right combination of tools (brainstorming, multi-voting, cause-effect diagram, and so on), facilitators can help groups work through the first four steps of the problem-solving process in as little as 30 minutes. With practice, groups can both solve problems more quickly and increase the odds that the solutions will be successful.

Making decisions

In the course of planning projects and solving problems, groups make hundreds of decisions. Some are minor, the responsibility of only one group member. Others are major, requiring commitment from every group member. Individuals can make decisions more quickly than groups. New groups struggle with making decisions unless they create a process for doing so. Following is a simple four-step process facilitators can use to help groups make decisions.

The first step in making a decision is to define what is to be decided. Some groups get stuck trying to make a decision because they do not take time to do this step. It may seem trivial or obvious, but it is really a critical step that is skipped too often. We have observed groups go in circles for 20 minutes while they wrestled with a decision—only to find that they did not even agree about the decision they were trying to make! Such a struggle is not necessarily a bad thing because groups learn from these experiences. Nevertheless, facilitators can help groups avoid falling into an unproductive pattern when it is time to make a decision by reminding them to start their process with this first step.

The second step in making a decision is to choose who will make it. Some decisions are best made by individuals, whereas other decisions require full participation by all group members. Regardless of who makes the decision, a group must agree to stand behind it. Knowing that a decision will be supported, whether it is made by one group member or the entire group, makes it easier to complete this second step in the decision-making process.

The Charter provides a quick way to determine who should be involved in making a decision. If a decision can be linked to a goal or role, then the person or persons accountable are readily identified from the Charter.

If the Charter does not identify the people who need to make a decision, then a quick discussion about who may be affected by the decision is helpful. If the group feels that relatively few people will be affected by it, then it can be made by one or two people. If the group feels that a decision will affect a relatively large number of people, then more group members should participate in making it. Consulting with those affected by the decision usually brings to light additional information that may need to be considered.

The third step in making decisions is to determine the criteria. Criteria are standards of judgment. When the criteria are clear, it is more likely that a decision will produce the desired outcome. A management group that was deciding which research projects to fund established the following decision-making criteria: The chosen projects would have the most positive impact on the organization's mission, total capital equipment budget for all projects would be less than $8 million, not more than one-quarter of the total research budget would be dedicated to technology new to the organization. They evaluated each project against each of these three criteria in order to choose the projects they would fund.

Individuals apply their own criteria to every decision they make, whether or not they are aware of it. Groups often get stuck in their decision-making process because they fail to agree on criteria or because they fail to set any criteria. Facilitators help prevent this problem by asking the group to determine their criteria for decision making.

The fourth step is to actually make the decision. Setting a deadline and choosing the decision-making tool is the way to complete this fourth and final step. Once the first three steps have been completed, one of the tools (from the tool box at the end of this chapter) is used to make the decision. Following are questions facilitators ask groups to help them work through this process and make decisions:

1. What are you going to decide?
2. Who will make the decision?
3. What criteria will you use to make your decision?
4. Who is affected by your decision?
5. When must you make your decision?
6. What tool will you use to make your decision?
7. What is your decision at this time?

The ultimate objective of planning and solving problems is to finish work. Finishing work—literally declaring it to be done—is the third fundamental work process.

Finishing work

Helping a group finish its work—sometimes referred to as reaching or achieving closure—is one of the most important things facilitators do. With so much work to do, groups often forget to acknowledge what they have accomplished. As soon as one task is complete, another takes its place. Busy groups can get so caught up in setting and achieving goals that they forget to step back, even for a moment, and look at what they have accomplished. This can drain the energy from a group, leading to a loss in productivity.

What does "finishing work" look like? Fulfilling the purpose of a meeting, completing an action step, finalizing a plan, solving a problem, or making a decision are all examples of finishing work. Completing goals from the Charter and ultimately fulfilling its purpose are also examples of finishing work. Facilitators help groups use their Charter to determine when they have or have not finished their work by asking questions such as:

1. Have you achieved the overall goal of this work? Is this work finished?

2.a. If not, what else needs to be done? Do action steps remain that need to be completed? Do new action steps need to be added?

   b. If so, what measures or other evidence do you have that the goal is accomplished or the work is done?

3. What have you learned from doing this work?

4. How can you formally declare this work done?

5. How can you recognize your accomplishments and celebrate your successes?

Many groups are not used to being asked by a facilitator about accomplishing their goals and finishing their work. The first time a group working for a small Internet service provider was challenged in this way by its facilitator, the discussion generated some heat. One member responded, "You are supposed to be working for us. Who are you to ask us how we know the broadcast e-mail system is working properly?" The facilitator replied, "I apologize if it sounded like I was interrogating you. I don't have much experience with your group and I am just curious about how you know your broadcast e-mail system is functioning properly. I'm wondering what measures you use to tell you about the performance of your software." This kind of highly energetic response on the part of a group member is often a sign that the work is not really finished, or that the goal was not clear in the first place. In this case, the group had not yet installed its performance monitoring system, and the group member responsible was feeling pressured and embarrassed about not being done yet. The facilitator helped the group put a plan in place to finish this part of the work.

Helping a group achieve closure on its work contributes to its performance and interdependence. Achieving goals that contribute to fulfilling the group's purpose and the organization's mission is what good group performance is all about. Acknowledging the contributions of individuals and members meets an important human need: to feel appreciated. Facilitators are in a good position to help groups recognize what they have accomplished.

Effective meetings

We define meetings very broadly as *two or more people getting together to discuss or do their work.* Defined in this way, it is safe to say that most people spend a significant time in meetings. Running effective meetings offers groups and their organizations a major opportunity to improve their productivity.

What is an effective meeting? It is one in which the purpose is accomplished in the time allotted. Good facilitators know how to help groups plan and run effective meetings. They create an environment where work can get done.

The average manager spends as much as half of his or her work time in meetings. Organizations that we have surveyed report that as many as half of such meetings are unproductive. This means that managers are wasting up to 25% of their time in poorly run meetings. By running effective meetings, managers could get back 10 hours of productive work time every week.

We have found two major causes of bad meetings: (1) the belief that meetings themselves are a waste of time and (2) poor meeting habits on the part of individuals.

Some people have experienced so many bad meetings that they have come to believe that nearly any meeting is a waste of time. This leads them to use poor meeting habits, thereby eliminating any chance of being productive during their meetings. These poor habits include not preparing adequately, arriving late, not listening to others, not following the agenda, and leaving early.

One manager of a marketing group had become so frustrated with the poor quality of his group meetings that he canceled them. He told the group, "Since most of us feel that these meetings are a waste of time, I see no reason to continue them. Let's go three months without having any of these formal, weekly group meetings and see what happens."

At first the group was elated. But after a few weeks, they noticed some problems. Important reviews of art copy and keylines, which used to occur in the weekly group meetings, were not getting done on time. Mistakes on promotional materials were slipping by the copyeditor. The manager and his group decided to try their weekly meeting process again, but this time to run the meetings differently.

They agreed to focus the weekly meetings on sharing information and reviewing the status of all their projects. Group members were given five minutes each to summarize their areas. People agreed to come prepared, and the weekly meetings were transformed into a brisk, efficient use of time. Because keyline reviews and copyediting involved only some of the group members, these meetings were held at a different time. How did the group accomplish this change? They used a simple process: Purpose–Agenda–Logistics (PAL).

Purpose–Agenda–Logistics (PAL) process for effective meetings

The first step in the PAL meeting process is to define the purpose of the meeting. Facilitators use clarifying questions to help a group do this. Being clear about the purpose is vital to having an effective meeting. In some cases, the purpose is mainly to share information. In other cases, a decision needs to be made or a plan outlined. Some meetings are designed to generate a number of options for solving a particular problem. Effective facilitators help groups get into the habit of developing clear purpose statements for their meetings and sticking to the agenda. Once the meeting purpose is established, facilitators help a group determine who needs to attend.

Setting an agenda is the second step in the PAL meeting process. The agenda is driven by the purpose of the meeting. The agenda points out who is responsible for different items. It also must describe a realistic amount of work that can be accomplished in the time available. Groups that are geographically dispersed feel particularly pressured to get a lot done while they are together because they meet infrequently. This can lead to members stuffing the agenda too full, hurrying through the meeting, and not doing a quality job on any one item. Facilitators help groups set realistic agendas by asking:

1. How will this agenda item contribute to fulfilling the purpose of the meeting?
2. Have you given yourself adequate time to accomplish the purpose of the meeting?

3. Can you schedule more time for this meeting, or do you need to eliminate one or more agenda items?

Setting up logistics is the third step in the PAL meeting process. Once the purpose and agenda are clear, it is important to plan for audiovisual support, appropriate meeting space and setting, food, and other facility needs. When meeting logistics work well, they tend to go unnoticed. When they don't work well, they can wreck a meeting and waste time. Facilitators contribute to successful meetings by helping groups take time to determine logistics requirements.

Figure 7-1 (page 118) shows a sample PAL meeting plan. A number of companies have adopted the PAL process, and they are more productive because of it. People in these companies actually look forward to meetings because the meetings help their groups make progress on their goals. They have established an organization norm: Employees use the PAL process. If they do not, people will not want to attend their meetings. New employees learn the PAL process through training and know that using it is required.

Effective meetings contribute to both interdependence and performance

A Fully Functioning Group, as described by the Group Development Curve, produces a high quantity and quality of work. Its members have a strong sense of interdependence. People are most satisfied when their tasks are meaningful and their social needs as human beings are being met. Some meetings are oriented to helping group members strengthen their interdependence, and others are oriented to contributing to performance. Although a meeting might be more oriented to one aspect of group development than the other, both things are always going on simultaneously.

For example, if the purpose of a 1-hour meeting is to share the individual work history of group members, the orientation of the meeting is clearly more toward building interdependence. Sharing this information helps the group understand the capabilities of individuals and the group as a whole. They will assign projects and devise steps with a better understanding of who can do what. This type of meeting also provides the group an opportunity to work on its performance. People have to come to the meeting prepared. They have to

Figure 7-1   Sample PAL meeting plan

R&D Project Funding Meeting

PURPOSE	LOGISTICS
Decide which R&D projects will be funded next year.	**Person calling this meeting:** Vice President, R&D
	Meeting date: October 25
	Time: 8:00 A.M. to 11:30 A.M.
	Location: Oakwood Conference Center
	Meeting materials: Funding criteria, current projects list
	AV equipment: Overhead, easels w/ flipcharts, water-based markers
	Food/Beverages: Continental breakfast by cafeteria; coffee and fruit for break
	Room layout: U-shape for 12 people

AGENDA

Start Time	End Time	Agenda Item	Lead
7:30 A.M.	8:00 A.M.	Continental breakfast	
8:00 A.M.	8:15 A.M.	Check in/review meeting purpose	Facilitator
8:15 A.M.	9:00 A.M.	Review funding criteria	V.P.
9:00 A.M.	10:00 A.M.	Review current projects and brainstorm new projects	Facilitator
10:00 A.M.	10:15 A.M.	Break	
10:15 A.M.	11:00 A.M.	Prioritize all projects using funding criteria	Facilitator
11:00 A.M.	11:15 A.M.	Reality check—see if we missed anything	Facilitator
11:15 A.M.	11:30 A.M.	Set next steps / close meeting	Facilitator

Participants: See attached list.

share their information efficiently if they hope to fulfill the purpose of the meeting in one hour. This meeting provides the group with an opportunity to increase members' interdependence and improve the group's performance. This combination can happen in every meeting.

Effective facilitators are masters at process, but are not ruled by it

The best facilitators have a knack for pulling out the right tool at the right time. They know when to use a highly structured approach and when to suggest something less structured. Their ability to accurately judge what a group needs comes from their use of the Facilitation Model. Facilitators with a clear understanding of the group's Task, who also use information at the Self and Group level, use tools effectively.

Effective facilitators are very proficient with tools and techniques. They practice the tools and use them with confidence. This confidence comes from preparation, practice, and past successes. Groups respond to this confidence and willingly work with facilitators who know what they are doing.

Effective facilitators are "light on their feet," however. They make spontaneous adjustments to the process in about half of the meetings they facilitate. When one tool does not yield the desired result, they try another. Facilitators who do not show this kind of flexibility often do more harm than good. Consider the comments made by a manager whose group had a terrible experience with a facilitator who was too stuck on his process:

"We had an important meeting where we had to prioritize a number of projects. On the first cut, we wanted to eliminate the projects we flat out would not fund. On the second cut, we wanted to prioritize the remaining projects because we knew that the projects at the bottom of the list also might not get funded. We set our prioritization criteria in advance of the meeting.

"The first part of the meeting went beautifully. We easily completed a sorting process using the multi-voting tool. But things fell apart in the second half of the meeting. The facilitator insisted we revisit our criteria before multi-voting again. I think the intent was good. He wanted us to make sure we were clear about the criteria. We felt a brief discussion would be sufficient, but he insisted we start from scratch with brainstorming the criteria. We argued about process for 30 minutes. We did not get our work done and some people in my group don't ever want to use a facilitator again."

This facilitator was hired because he was known to be very good at using tools. He was so invested in his choice of tools, however, that he failed to help the group accomplish its task. He did not use the clear signals from the group to make adjustments. He was so certain he was right that he was unable to perceive other ways of getting the work done. The damage was not contained to the meeting, either. This was a cross-functional team with part-time members who reported to other functional managers. They were put behind in their schedule because they could not reconvene for several days. It took a while for the group to regain its momentum.

Contrast this experience with that of an executive group charged with developing a new strategic plan for the organization. During the group's second 90-minute meeting, the facilitator proposed that the group complete a force field analysis to document the forces for change and forces for stability that were acting on the organization. This information would be used to make sure that the strategic goals and key initiatives accounted for these forces. The group first brain-stormed a list of forces. To get a sense of the relative strength of these forces, the facilitator asked them to multi-vote on the list because this had worked well with other groups.

The group did not like the suggestion. Members felt that such an exercise would take too much time and not yield the desired result. Instead, they proposed that they just have a general discussion about the forces. They believed that the discussion would accomplish two things in less time: They would develop a common understanding of the forces and end up with a ranking of their relative strength. They were right. The facilitator adjusted and the group had a lively debate about the forces. They accomplished both of their objectives.

The president of the organization later remarked to the facilitator, "We have worked hard to draft an agenda for every one of these work sessions and we always end up making changes 'live and in color' right during the meeting. I'm glad you can do that, because I always have a moment of panic when it happens." The facilitator let the president know that she also "got an adrenaline rush" at those moments when the process had to be revamped during the course of the meeting. She remarked, "I do that more than half of the time. I have a lot of experience with your group, and I trust that the members know what to do." The facilitator's experience making adjustments during meetings and her expertise with tools gave her the flexibility she needed to help groups get where they wanted to go.

Different situations require different tools

Effective facilitators understand the situational nature of their role. They understand that a tool or technique that is helpful in one case might not work as well in a second, apparently identical case. They also know when to stick with an agenda and when to adjust it in response to what is happening with the group.

How do facilitators know how and when to intervene? What is the right facilitation tool for a given situation? Effective facilitators use their knowledge of both the group and its task to choose facilitation tools, share observations, or offer guidance. Based on past experience, facilitators know which tools work well in different situations. While facilitating a work session, effective facilitators use information at the Self and Group level to determine how their interventions are supporting or interfering with the group's progress. Good facilitators then make adjustments as needed.

The tool box

Effective facilitators choose different tools depending on the task the group wants to accomplish. We use all of these tools for the three fundamental work processes. We have purposely not included tools like histograms, control charts, and scatter diagrams because they are not tools we use while facilitating work sessions. Nevertheless, such tools can be useful to groups, especially for reporting information. Based upon our own experiences and on our surveys of other facilitators, we have chosen nine tools that we find are used the most.

The Tool Box

Tool	Objective for Using	Page
Brainstorming	Generate as many ideas as possible.	123
Consensus	Gain commitment to support a group action or decision.	124
Process mapping	Describe and illustrate a process in a step-by-step sequence.	125
Parking lot	Record items that would divert the group from its current task, but that need to be considered later.	126
Multi-voting	Sort a list and/or reduce the number of items on a list.	127
Affinity diagram	Quickly organize a large list of ideas.	128
Cause-effect diagram	Identify and organize information about possible causes of a problem or desired outcome (observed effect).	129
Force field analysis	Illustrate the forces for change and forces for stability that are influencing a situation.	130
Debrief	Describe or evaluate the completion of a task, activity, or experience.	131

Explanation of tool format

Objective:	The main objective of using this tool
Summary:	A general description of the tool; typical situations; common pitfalls
Guidelines:	The guidelines for using this tool—general recommendations; things to keep in mind when using this tool
Steps:	The fundamental "how to" of using the tool, step by step
Options:	Optional steps and suggestions for different materials or approaches that can help tool use
Group development:	How using the tool can help the group work together better

Brainstorming

Objective:	Generate as many ideas as possible.
Summary:	A good brainstorming session produces a long list of ideas. Groups use brainstorming more than any other tool. When a group wants to consider all possibilities, come up with new ideas, and expand beyond current thinking, brainstorming is a good place to start.

Guidelines:

- Everyone is encouraged to produce as many ideas as possible.
- Quantity is the goal, *so do not judge others' ideas.*
- Record ideas so everyone can see them.

Steps:

1. Decide how to use the information—have a purpose for brainstorming.
2. Read the brainstorming guidelines to the group.
3. Give everyone approximately 5 minutes to silently work alone to generate some ideas.
4. Invite everyone to share his or her ideas and record them exactly as they are spoken.
5. Stop the session when no one has any more ideas. Be willing to wait through several silent periods so people can think. Do not cut them off too soon.

Options:

- You can record ideas on index cards or removable notes so they can be moved around and grouped together later.
- You may want to use "nominal group technique" if more vocal group members are dominating the session. In nominal group technique, people take turns, sharing their ideas one at a time until all ideas have been heard.
- When recording ideas on flipcharts, you may want to have two people recording ideas to keep things moving at a fast pace.

Group development:

Brainstorming helps people in a group get better at listening to one another. It also helps groups value and support input from every group member. Some people have a tendency to judge ideas quickly. Following the guidelines of brainstorming gives them practice at listening and suspending judgment. They can learn new behavior while helping the group get its work done.

Brainstorming also helps people build on the ideas of others—a practical example of the synergy that can come from effective group work.

Consensus

Objective:	Gain commitment to support a group action or decision.
Summary:	When a group reaches consensus, it means that all members agree to support a group action. Members might not completely agree with the action, but they do agree to support it, both within and outside of the group. Consensus is *not* a majority vote. New groups have a tendency to use the consensus tool too frequently. Some actions or decisions can still be made by individuals or by voting. The group's Charter will help them know when consensus is required.

Guidelines:
- Use when the commitment of all group members is required. If such commitment is not required, consider alternatives to consensus such as individual decision making or majority vote.
- Use when the group is creating a win–win or compromise solution.

Steps:
1. Clearly define the action or decision through discussion.
2. Agree that consensus is required.
3. Ask the group the following questions:
   a. Can you live with this action?
   b. Will you support this action within the group?
   c. Will you support this action outside of the group?

   If anyone is unable to answer yes to any of the questions, then ask her or him to answer the following question:

   d. What has to change in order for you to support this action?
4. Confirm that the group has reached consensus.

Options:
- Put a time limit on discussion. If consensus is not reached, use the Conflict Resolution Process.

Group development: Using the consensus tool is an effective way of helping group members achieve the group's goal rather than always having it their way. It improves both productivity and interdependence.

Process mapping

Objective: Describe and illustrate a process in a step-by-step sequence.

Summary: Process maps accurately show the steps of a work process, providing a clear picture of how the process works. The purpose should be clear before the work is done. The discussion and debate that occurs during a process mapping session is just as valuable as the final process map. Groups discover: (1) The process is not always done the same way; (2) some steps are wasteful and easily can be eliminated; (3) bottlenecks; (4) steps that are not being done; and (5) other trouble spots. Process maps are also called flowcharts.

Guidelines:
- Note where the group disagrees because that is where problems usually occur in the process.
- Identify "owners"—those people responsible for certain parts of the process.

Steps:
1. Determine the purpose for doing the process map.
2. Produce a 1–2 sentence definition of the process.
3. Determine the level of detail that the process map will show. Allow for some variation.
4. Identify the beginning and end points.
5. Have owners map their part of the process in front of the group.
6. Confirm that the process has been accurately mapped with the consensus tool.
7. Take a look at the entire process. Ask the following questions:
   a. Does every part of the process have an owner?
   b. Where are there discrepancies in the process?
   c. Where are there the biggest bottlenecks or quality problems?
   d. Can some steps be eliminated?
8. Determine the next steps; confirm how the process map will be used.

Options:
- Record each process step on a large index card or removable note so it can be moved around later—groups will debate the sequence of steps. Trying to flipchart the process directly is too messy.
- Identify measures (existing or new) that indicate how well the process is functioning.
- Once a process has been mapped, ask the group to map an "ideal" process.

Group development: Completing a process map helps people improve their listening skills. It helps people understand how their part of the process helps the group.

Parking lot

Objective: Record items that would divert the group from its current task, but that need to be considered later.

Summary: The "parking lot" is a list of items that will be dealt with at a later time. During a meeting, topics come up that are important but not related to the current task or meeting. Or, more information is needed before the discussion can proceed. In these cases, items can be put on the parking lot. This helps groups stay focused on the purpose of a work session.

Guidelines:
- The parking lot acknowledges that the issue raised is important, but will be dealt with later.
- Specify a time to return to the parking lot.
- The parking lot should *not* be used to shut down opposing points of view about the current task.

Steps:
1. Put the words "Parking Lot" at the top of a flip-chart.
2. Explain how the parking lot is used, if the group does not already know.
3. Place appropriate items on the parking lot.
4. At the end of the meeting, specify a later time to deal with items from the parking lot.

Options:
- A group member can record an item on the parking lot without immediately announcing it to the group.
- Individuals recording items on the parking lot can be asked to take responsibility for bringing the item up to the group later.

Group development: Using the parking lot helps a group honor the ideas put forth by its members. People feel that they have been heard and the group stays on task, which contributes to higher productivity and a stronger sense of interdependence.

Multi-voting

Objective: Sort a list and/or reduce the number of items on a list.

Summary: Multi-voting is a simple and quick tool that helps a group sort a list or reduce the number of items on a list. It can be used to work with the information generated during a brainstorming session. When used to sort a list, it helps a group get a general sense of priority. When used to reduce a list, each round of multi-voting cuts the list roughly in half. Multi-voting is *not* a very analytical tool.

Guidelines:
- Each member is given the same number of votes.
- The number of votes for each group member is equal to a third to a half of the total number of items on the list. For example, if the list contains 30 items, then each person gets 10–15 votes.

Steps:
1. Decide whether the group is sorting or reducing the list, or both.
2. Look for opportunities to combine similar items.
3. Agree on the voting criteria. The group may have to use the consensus tool to do this. For example, the criterion for voting on a list of projects might be, "Give more votes to the projects having the most impact on the group's purpose."
4. Agree on how votes can be distributed.
5. Assign the same number of votes to each person.
6. Give the group 2–5 minutes to work silently and individually to decide how to cast their votes.
7. Cast the votes.
8. Total the results and sort or reduce the list. Decide whether to conduct another round of multi-voting.

Options:
- Some groups find it helpful to number the items on the list before multi-voting.
- Some situations call for multi-voting by secret ballot. A simple show of hands is OK in other situations. A third option is to have everyone mark their votes silently on the same flipchart.
- Set some guidelines for the maximum number of votes allowed per item. For example, 15 votes could be distributed as follows: 5 for the first choice, 4 for the second choice, 3 for the third, 2 for the fourth, and 1 for the fifth. Or, people can cast all of their votes for one item, if they so desire.

Group development: Multi-voting helps every member of a group participate. This leads to a greater level of commitment by group members.

Affinity diagram

Objective: Quickly organize a large list of ideas.

Summary: An affinity diagram helps quickly organize a large list of ideas. It is especially useful for organizing lists of 30 or more items.

Guidelines:
- The first step in using this tool is usually brainstorming, so the brainstorming guidelines apply.
- Sorting steps should be conducted silently.
- The same item can be placed in more than one category during the sorting steps.

Steps:
1. Decide why you are using this tool and how the information will be used.
2. Conduct a brainstorming session. Put the items on note cards or removable notes.
3. Have people get up and come to where the cards or notes are displayed and silently sort the items, grouping like items together.
4. If two or more people think an item belongs in more than one grouping, make a duplicate and put the item in both groupings.
5. After 5–15 minutes of silent sorting, have the group discuss the groupings.
6. Choose a heading that best describes each grouping. The heading name usually can be found on one of the items in a given grouping, although it is OK to create a heading that is not already within the grouping.
7. Record the final results.

Options:
- If the group is larger than 6–8 people, divide the group in two (call them groups A and B) for the sorting process. Have group A silently sort for 5–10 minutes while group B observes. Then have the groups switch roles, with B sorting and A observing. Choosing the headings can be done either in two groups or one large group.
- If necessary, use a decision-making process, consensus, or Conflict Resolution Process to work out differences of opinion.

Group development: Using this tool gives a group practice at organizing large amounts of information as a first step in solving more complex problems. This gives them confidence in dealing with some larger problems later.

Cause-effect diagram

Objective: Identify and organize information about possible causes of a problem or desired outcome (observed effect).

Summary: The cause-effect diagram illustrates the possible causes of a problem or desired outcome. Arranging information using this tool leads to a better under-standing of the factors contributing to an observed effect. This better understanding helps the group evaluate a number of factors before jumping to solutions too quickly. Cause-effect diagrams help groups identify what data they may need to understand the cause of a problem and solve it.

Guidelines:
- The first step in using this tool is usually brain-storming, so the brainstorming guidelines apply.

Steps:
1. Decide why you are using this tool and how the information will be used.
2. Conduct a brainstorming session. Brainstorm the possible causes of an observed effect. Put the items on note cards or removable notes.
3. Have people get up and come to where the cards or notes are displayed. Silently sort the items, grouping like items together.
4. If two or more people think an item belongs in more than one grouping, make a duplicate and put the item in both groupings.
5. After 5–15 minutes of silent sorting, have the group discuss the groupings.
6. Choose a heading that best describes each group-ing. The heading name usually can be found on one of the items in a given grouping, although it is OK to create a heading that is not already within the grouping.
7. Record the final results.
8. Choose causes to investigate. Focus on the most impactful causes.

Options:
- You can provide the categories at the beginning of the brainstorming session and then brainstorm items under each. Categories used include: meth-ods, materials, machinery, and people.
- The output of an affinity diagram can easily be reformatted as a cause-effect diagram.

Group development: Using this tool gives a group practice at organizing large amounts of information as a first step in solving more complex problems. It helps groups feel more confident in their ability to understand complex problems and identify the actions they can take.

Force field analysis

Objective:	Illustrate the forces for change and forces for stability that are influencing a situation.
Summary:	A good force field analysis helps a group make plans to create something new from a current situation. Moving from the current state to a new state requires an understanding of forces for change and forces for stability. These forces provide information about "leverage points" for changing a situation. A force field analysis is a good place to start when considering less concrete or tangible situations.
Guidelines:	• Make sure the group develops a plan or simple set of action steps after completing the analysis. • Groups identify forces for change more easily than they do forces for stability. You may have to prompt them with questions.
Steps:	1. Decide how this information will be used. 2. Describe the current state or situation. 3. Describe the desired future state or situation. 4. Identify the forces that will compel us to change (called *forces for change* or *driving forces*). 5. Identify the forces that will compel us to remain the same (called *forces for stability* or *restraining forces*). 6. Set action steps to enhance driving forces and reduce restraining forces.
Options:	• Brainstorming is a good tool to use with steps 4 and 5. • Forces for stability, or restraining forces, are hard to identify because they are part of the taken-for-granted assumptions. Have the group use the elements of a paradigm (behaviors/activities, vocabulary, assumptions/beliefs, values) to help the group identify these forces.
Group development:	Groups gain experience and skill in solving more complex problems. They also feel their ability to manage change more effectively as a result of using this tool, as long as they set action steps and follow through.

Debrief

Objective:	Describe or evaluate the completion of a task, activity, or experience.
Summary:	Debriefing helps groups learn about how its members are working together and what they can do to improve.
Guidelines:	• Give every group member the opportunity to participate in the debriefing discussion. • Groups should agree to hold debriefing discussions at the completion of significant tasks or projects.
Steps:	Debriefing is facilitated by asking the following questions: 1. What was your experience when you were working on this task? 2. What went well? 3. What did not go well? 4. How can you do things differently next time?
Options:	• Let people take some notes before beginning the discussion. • Use nominal group technique to conduct the discussion. In nominal group technique, people take turns, sharing their ideas one at a time until all ideas have been heard. • Specify a time limit or range (with a minimum and maximum time set aside for the debrief) for conducting this discussion.
Group development:	Debriefing may be the most important group development tool. It facilitates learning about how group members work together and contributes to their interdependence.

C H A P T E R   8

Active Listening: The Most Important Facilitation Skill

In this chapter you will learn:

- How to improve your active listening skills
- How to ask questions effectively
- About common barriers to listening and how to overcome them
- About your current listening skills

*A*ctive listening is by far the most important facilitation skill. A facilitator who cannot listen well is no facilitator at all. Groups that are dissatisfied with a facilitator's services inevitably report that the individual "just did not listen." Only by listening effectively can you:

- Interpret what task the group wants to complete
- Get clear signals that give you insight about how a group is working
- Be aware of particular dynamics that affect a group's productivity and interdependence
- Know how well a work process is going
- Get information about the changes occurring within the group
- Understand boundaries that are coming into play at any given moment.

Listening is a skill that can be acquired and improved. In this chapter, we provide practical things for you to do to improve your listening skills.

L istening self-assessment

We provide a very simple listening self-assessment on the following two pages. Facilitators have found it useful in gauging their own listening skills over time. After using the active listening process, using open-ended questions and working to overcome common barriers to listening, facilitators find that their scores increase.

Listening Self-Assessment

Choose one response for each of the items below. Base your choice on what you usually do, not on what you think a facilitator *should* do.

1. When you are going to lunch with a friend, you:
   a. Focus your attention on the menu and then on the service provided
   b. Ask about events in your friend's life and pay attention to what's said
   c. Exchange summaries of what is happening to each of you while focusing attention on the meal

2. When someone talks nonstop, you:
   a. Ask questions at an appropriate time in an attempt to help the person focus on the issue
   b. Make an excuse to end the conversation
   c. Try to be patient and understand what you are being told

3. If a group member complains about a fellow employee who, you believe, is disrupting the group, you:
   a. Pay attention and withhold your opinions
   b. Share your own experiences and feelings about that employee
   c. Acknowledge the group member's feelings and ask the group member what options he or she has

4. If someone is critical of you, you:
   a. Try not to react or get upset
   b. Automatically become curious and attempt to learn more
   c. Listen attentively and then back up your position

5. You are having a very busy day and someone tells you to change the way you are completing a task. You believe the person is wrong, so you:
   a. Thank her or him for the input and keep doing what you were doing
   b. Try to find out why she or he thinks you should change
   c. Acknowledge that the other may be right, tell her or him you are very busy, and agree to follow up later

6. When you are ready to respond to someone else, you:
   a. Sometimes will interrupt the person if you believe it is necessary
   b. Almost always speak before the other is completely finished talking
   c. Rarely offer your response until you believe the other has finished

7. After a big argument with someone you have to work with every day, you:
   a. Settle yourself and then try to understand the other's point of view before stating your side again
   b. Just try to go forward and let bygones be bygones
   c. Continue to press your position

8. A colleague calls to tell you that he is upset about getting assigned to a new job. You decide to:
   a. Ask him if he can think of options to help him deal with the situation
   b. Assure him that he is good at what he does and that these things have a way of working out for the best
   c. Let him know you have heard how badly he feels

9. If a friend always complains about her problems but never asks about yours, you:
   a. Try to identify areas of common interest
   b. Remain understanding and attentive, even if it becomes tedious
   c. Support her complaints and mention your own complaints

10. The best way to remain calm in an argument is to:
    a. Continue to repeat your position in a firm but even manner
    b. Repeat what you believe is the other person's position
    c. Tell the other person that you are willing to discuss the matter again when you are both calmer

Score each item of your Listening Self-Assessment

1. (a) 0	(b) 10	(c) 5	**6.** (a) 5	(b) 0	(c) 10
2. (a) 10	(b) 0	(c) 5	**7.** (a) 10	(b) 5	(c) 0
3. (a) 5	(b) 0	(c) 5	**8.** (a) 5	(b) 5	(c) 10
4. (a) 5	(b) 10	(c) 0	**9.** (a) 0	(b) 10	(c) 5
5. (a) 0	(b) 10	(c) 5	**10.** (a) 0	(b) 10	(c) 5

Add up your total score

80–100   **You are an active, excellent listener.** You achieve a good balance between listening and asking questions, and you strive to understand others.

50–75   **You are an adequate-to-good listener.** You listen well, although you may sometimes react too quickly to others before they are finished speaking.

25–45   You have some listening skills but need to improve them. You may often become impatient when trying to listen to others, hoping they will finish talking so you can talk.

0–20   You listen to others very infrequently. You may prefer to do all of the talking and experience extreme frustration while waiting for others to make their point.

What is active listening?

Active listening is a process by which we make a conscious effort to understand someone else. *Effective facilitators are active listeners.* They strive to listen effectively and consciously manage their process. The active listening process is:

1. *Sensing:* Using all of your senses to take in information
2. *Interpreting:* Evaluating the meaning of the information
3. *Checking:* Reflecting on what you have heard in an effort to gain a mutual understanding of the speaker's intended message

Sensing

Sensing is the first step in the listening process. It is a data-gathering activity. We use all of our senses to take in information. We usually do this automatically and unconsciously. Effective listeners raise this data gathering to a conscious level. When beginning a conversation, they remind themselves to make the speakers important, and pay attention to cues that will help them better understand the message the speakers are trying to deliver.

A facilitator was helping a sales group complete its annual budget. One of the group's account executives had just agreed to a significant increase in her sales quota. The group had asked her if she thought the increase was possible, and she said, "Yes, I think we can do it." At that point, she stopped offering suggestions about other budget items. She put her chin in the palm of her hand and leaned against the arm of her chair.

What was the account executive saying? A good active listener pays attention to verbal, vocal, and visual cues. Such cues paint a clearer, more complete picture of the speaker's intended meaning. Verbal information is literally the words used by the speaker. Vocal information is the tone, rate, and volume in which those words are spoken. Visual information includes things like body language and facial expressions. Surprisingly, we get as much or more information from vocal and visual cues as we do from verbal cues.

Interpreting

Interpreting is the second step in the listening process. As we take in information, we evaluate and analyze it. Again, we usually do this automatically and unconsciously. Effective listeners also raise this step in the process to a conscious level. When interpreting information, they strive to understand the meaning the speaker intends. They eliminate the barriers that make it difficult to accurately interpret the speaker. We discuss these barriers and what to do to overcome them later in this chapter.

The account executive mentioned above was sending some strong signals about the new sales quota she had agreed to. The facilitator believed the account executive was troubled by it. He looked for an opportunity to discuss the new quota further.

Checking

Checking is the third and final step in the active listening process. Checking requires thinking first, then making reflective statements and asking questions of the speaker to clarify what has been said. Reflective statements convey the meaning the listener gave to the message. Such statements usually begin as follows: "What I heard you say was . . ." Reflective statements tell the speaker, "Here is what I think you mean."

Good listeners ask helpful questions as they check with the speaker. These questions usually are open-ended to encourage people to provide more information. Table 8-1 (page 138) shows examples of four different types of open-ended questions active listeners use. Good listeners resist the temptation to advise, criticize, or judge when asking these questions. They use these questions because they are genuinely curious to find out what other people mean.

Table 8-1   Open-ended questions

Question Type		Examples
Openers	Elicit general information that may lead to more specific questions	What are your ideas about your role in this group?
		What do you think are the goals of this project?
Follow-ups	Ask for elaboration, or to aid understanding	Would you please say some more about that?
		What was the result?
		What do you think can be improved?
Clarifiers	Gain a clearer understanding of what has been said	What do you mean by "urgent"?
		When you say you want this done "early next week," can you provide a day and time?
Probes	Generate more or different information	Anything else?
		What do you think are the possible responses to this action?

The account executive from the sales group let out a big sigh as the group returned from a break. The facilitator used this opportunity to check with her. "Do you have any ideas about the new sales quota for your territory?" he asked. The account executive replied, "I agreed to this quota because I really felt that saying no was not allowed. The truth is, this new quota would be 40% over last year's plan, which was a record year for us. I have some ideas about how to do this, but I am concerned about basing our budget on a revenue level that is so much higher than we have ever achieved." The group worked together to evaluate its options. The facilitator's question had brought to the surface a very important point. By actively listening and asking an open-ended question, the facilitator helped the group identify options they otherwise would not have considered.

To improve our ability to use the active listening process, it is important to understand the common barriers to active listening. These barriers can interfere with each step in the process. Effective facilitators are aware of these barriers and have taught themselves and others how to overcome them.

Barriers to effective listening

Perhaps the biggest barrier to effective listening is the unconscious nature of the process. We take listening for granted. We take in information with all of our senses constantly, and automatically give meaning to what we take in. It is easy to respond without thinking first. Some people use very little of their full listening capability because they do not consciously put more energy into it. The challenge for facilitators is to make their listening process work at 100% of its capacity. A practical way to do this is to remind yourself of the three steps to the active listening process. Aside from the unconscious nature of the process, there are other barriers that facilitators need to know about. In the following sections, we discuss some common barriers. Table 8-2 (page 140) describes what to do to overcome them.

Positive and negative triggers

Certain words and phrases can elicit an immediate emotional response. We call these words and phrases "triggers." Triggers for some people include "team player" and "total quality." For others, swearing is a trigger. A positive trigger is a word or phrase that creates good feelings for the listener ("Nice job!" "Thank you"). A negative trigger is a word or phrase that creates feelings such as anger or apathy. Triggers short-circuit the listening process. The listener, upon hearing just a few words, has a preprogrammed interpretation and response. Triggers cut off the data-gathering activities of the senses and can lead to a highly erroneous evaluation. Triggers interfere with listening because the listeners immediately turn their attention to the emotions they are experiencing. Effective facilitators identify their own triggers in order to gain conscious control of their actions and listen more effectively.

Word definition differences

Because experiences, family life, beliefs, knowledge, and so on are unique for each person, each of us has our own meaning for words.

Table 8-2   *What to do to overcome barriers to effective listening*

Barrier	What to Do About It
Positive triggers	1. Make a list of words or phrases that auto-matically make you feel good. 2. How do you feel when you hear these words or phrases? 3. Note your emotional and physical responses and use them as signals to alert you.
Negative triggers	1. Make a list of words or phrases that auto-matically make you feel bad. 2. How do you feel when you hear these words or phrases? 3. Note your emotional and physical responses and use them as signals to alert you. 4. Try to understand why these are negative triggers for you. Why do you react so strongly to the words or phrases? This will help you "reprogram" your response.
Word definition differences	1. Ask clarifying questions when you detect dif-ferences in word usage or definition.
Personal matters	1. Be aware of personal matters that are going on in your life. 2. Promise yourself, "I will take care of this after facilitating this work session." 3. Follow up on your promise to yourself.
Poor physical surroundings	1. View the meeting room before the meeting. Make sure the space will not prevent achiev-ing the meeting purpose. 2. Make sure you can see all of the partici-pants. 3. Move furniture around if you have to. 4. Noise is the biggest concern. Eliminate dis-tracting or loud noises if possible.
Fatigue	1. Rest before you facilitate. 2. If you are tired, schedule more frequent, shorter breaks. 3. Remind yourself of the active listening pro-cess while you facilitate, perhaps keeping a picture of it in front of you.
Filters	1. Make a list of your significant filters. 2. Ask yourself, "How does this filter interfere with my ability to listen?" 3. Be more conscious of your filters when you are trying to listen. Your heightened aware-ness will help you listen better.

No two people have exactly the same meaning for a given word or phrase. These differences can lead to minor misinterpretations or major misunderstandings. Effective facilitators check the meaning of words with the speaker and help groups develop consensus on the definition of important words and phrases.

A common problem area for groups is the many different meanings of the following terms: strategic plan, mission, vision, and goals. If you are asked to facilitate the development of a strategic plan, for instance, strongly encourage the group to define "strategic plan." Ask the group to identify how such a plan will be used. Push group members to agree on the format of the plan. Effective facilitators pay close attention to the vocabulary a group uses. A 5-minute discussion about the meaning of a particular word can prevent a group from wasting hours of work time later.

Personal matters

All of us have important personal matters outside of our work life. Sometimes these matters require a great deal of attention and take a lot of energy. It's tough to listen effectively at these times. Effective facilitators monitor the effects of their own personal matters and take time to deal with them. When it is time to listen, they consciously remind themselves to use the active listening process.

A manager who was going through a very difficult divorce found it hard to listen during meetings. His boss was very understanding and supportive, yet there were times when the manager had to put personal matters aside and meet his obligations to the organization. We helped the manager develop a useful device: a promise to himself to deal with his personal problems later. Just before facilitating his group's meetings, the manager would say to himself, "I acknowledge that this is a hard time for me. Doing my job well will help me feel better about myself and help my family stay secure. I promise to deal with this issue after this meeting. Now, I'm going to go in there and do a great job."

Key to the successful use of this device was following through on his promise to himself. In addition, the manager did not try to hide his feelings. He found that active listening helped him get in touch with his feelings. "I have learned how to get my work done in a variety of emotional states. I have also learned how to adjust my expectations of others as their emotions ebb and flow."

Poor physical surroundings

Sometimes physical surroundings interfere with listening. We have facilitated group work sessions in places that contribute to effective listening, such as excellent conference facilities and meeting rooms. We have also tried to facilitate meetings in noisy, distracting places such as construction sites and casinos. Noise level, lighting, room temperature, acoustics, and room layout are just a few of the things that can help or hinder listening. Effective facilitators plan ahead and take action to correct or minimize problems like these.

Fatigue

It is very difficult to listen when you are tired. Active listening takes an alert mind and a rested body. Effective facilitators try to get a good night's sleep prior to working with their groups. If they must facilitate a work session when fatigued, they create more frequent breaks and enlist the help of the group to keep track of what has been said.

Busy managers often do not feel rested. The fast pace of change and increasing demands on their time seem to drain their energy well before the end of the day. One manager with whom we consulted developed a real appreciation for the value of the active listening process. "Right after our baby was born, I never got more than four hours of sleep every night. I came to work feeling like a zombie nearly every day. The only way I was able to listen was to write down the active listening process on my calendar. I kept that list of questions handy, and I asked my staff to help me listen, too. It's really helped us communicate more clearly and avoid misunderstandings."

Filters

Filters interfere with active listening. These include things such as beliefs, assumptions, values, expectations, past experiences, and interests. Filters are subtle and thus hard to detect. For instance, I may believe that someone who is sitting quietly in a lively group meeting is not interested or engaged. Because of this belief, I might value participants who are more animated. I may even ignore quieter people and not listen to them well. Effective facilitators identify their own filters and prevent them from interfering in their listening process.

Good flipcharting techniques: Evidence of your listening skills

One of the ways facilitators demonstrate their ability to listen, and in the process help groups communicate more effectively, is flipcharting what people are saying. Good flipcharting techniques are essential. Some simple guidelines will make a big difference for your group. These include:

- Print legibly and big enough so everyone can see.
- Write down exactly what people say. Avoid the temptation to edit. You'll find this actually goes faster.
- If you feel you must edit, ask permission to do so. Check to see that your edit matches the intended meaning of the speaker.
- Write down everyone's comments. Don't screen out or be selective.
- Alternate colors on long lists. This is especially helpful during brainstorming.
- For shorter, more descriptive lists, make groupings similar in color.
- If the group is shouting out information faster than you can write it down, ask someone to help you.
- Prepare more complicated diagrams and tables in advance.

The most effective facilitators are active listeners. They work continuously to improve their listening skills. They approach every work session knowing they will listen more than talk. They remind themselves of the active listening process so they can take in information, interpret it, and check their interpretation. Effective facilitators strive to learn about their own personal barriers to listening so they can overcome them.

New Insights into Facilitation

With so much going on within a group setting—the work to complete the tasks and the many interactions among group members—facilitators must take great care in deciding how to help their groups. Part II provides new perspectives and helps facilitators choose the most effective actions.

Boundaries are a powerful and practical framework through which facilitators can examine various work situations (Chapter 9). We have grouped boundaries into four main types: boundaries *between individuals, how to work together* boundaries, *elements of work* boundaries, and *imposed* boundaries. Using the framework of boundaries provides facilitators a way to understand what is happening and take appropriate action.

No group completes its work without experiencing and/or creating **change**. It is through better understanding of how change occurs at the individual, group, and organizational level that facilitators can help people be more effective (Chapter 10). Facilitators need to attend to the impact of change on people because it has such a significant effect on their productivity. Facilitators also need to help groups be more effective in creating the changes they desire. In each of these areas, there are practical actions that facilitators can take.

Quick Fix, the final chapter of this book (Chapter 11), provides fast, comprehensive answers to 15 of the most common problems that facilitators have reported to us. Each Quick Fix provides insights into a particular problem, prescribes actions facilitators and groups can take, and indicates where to turn in this book for more information about different aspects of the problem.

Used in conjunction with the four essential elements that make up the Facilitation Model (Task, Self, Group, and Process), these new insights give facilitators a comprehensive and useful set of skills. People who master the Facilitation Model and apply their knowledge of boundaries and change can make significant contributions to their groups and organizations.

Facilitation Is Boundary Management

In this chapter you will learn:

- To define facilitation as boundary management
- Four types of boundaries
- Many boundaries that impact groups
- Ten boundaries requiring the most attention

A facilitator, working without a conscious awareness and clear understanding of boundaries, can look and feel like a person walking in a forest at night. In the dark of night a forest is unfamiliar and full of dangers. A person can lose the trail, get tangled in the undergrowth, and may even get smacked in the forehead by a low-hanging branch. Such a walk can be filled with frustration, anger, and even fear. An awareness of boundaries provides the light a facilitator needs for the journey. Understanding boundaries helps a facilitator avoid some of the bumps and bruises. Managing boundaries well creates productive, enjoyable experiences for facilitators and the groups they serve.

What are boundaries?

In the simplest terms, a boundary is something (a line, point, or plane) that indicates or fixes a limit or extent. In the context of groups, boundaries define a variety of limits for individuals and groups.

Everyone lives in a world defined by many different boundaries, and, most often, a person operates without conscious awareness of those boundaries. Awareness of a boundary usually arises when an individual or group bumps into it. They may be comforted by its presence, chafe at being blocked, or they may boldly step across the boundary and then have to deal with the consequences of their action. Some boundaries define the very work that is to be done. Boundaries may be defined by an individual, a group, organization, or the larger society. Whether they are consciously identified or not, boundaries affect nearly every aspect of a group's work.

Facilitators have some awareness of many of these boundaries, even if they don't call them "boundaries." They may be more familiar with terms like:

expectations	scope	norms
what's acceptable	limit of authority	ground rules
way we have done it	policies	laws

Why should boundaries be important to a facilitator?

Managing boundaries is fundamental to facilitation. In fact, much of the work of facilitators can be described in terms of boundaries. Boundaries affect the ways groups interact. Pushing (moving or modifying) them is a helpful way of framing much of a group's work. Thinking of these interactions and work as boundary management gives facilitators and groups a useful tool for being more successful.

Facilitators and groups face a wide variety of boundaries. Some have a greater impact and are more consciously negotiated, whereas others have less obvious impact. Boundaries define the limits of interactions between group members, how group members work with each other, fundamental elements of the work itself, and what constraints are imposed on the group from outside. Using the concept of boundaries enables group members to be more effective in working together, assess critical information about their environment, and successfully complete their work.

Naming boundaries provides a vocabulary for discussing topics and issues that a group would most likely avoid talking about because of the potential for conflict or simply because they did not think of it. Creating agreement on how to deal with these boundaries is a vital step in attaining the highest level of group productivity.

Nikita served as an important communication hub for her work group. Her work space was thus out in the open, so she could be easily reached. At times, however, Nikita needed quiet work time to publish marketing literature for the group. Because of her role and easy access, she was frequently interrupted by group members. Nikita found that she was frustrated and angry with her co-workers because of their lack of respect for her needs, but she also felt she might be labeled "not a team player" if she spoke up.

After learning about boundary management at a seminar, Nikita suddenly found she had a vocabulary for discussing her experiences and feelings about this situation. In a group meeting, she pointed out that the group's ignoring her need for occasional quiet time violated her *space boundary*. One co-worker's frequent removal of items from her desk without permission was, in fact, violating her *property boundary*. With these descriptions, the group was able to understand her concerns and make adjustments.

In actively managing boundaries, groups are able to more clearly know which boundaries need to be defined, which ones honored, and which ones pushed if the group is to be successful. Pushing a boundary means actively working to change it or, in some situations, ignoring it. A facilitator plays a critical role in helping a group discern which boundaries need to be pushed or honored in order to be most productive.

Sarah, the project group leader, was feeling steamed again. The group had just listed the next set of tasks to be completed and several group members had once again agreed to do a minimal amount of work. Sarah could see they were going to end another meeting with important work still unassigned. In the past, she had ended up doing it. She was tired of working the extra hours while others always went home on time. She felt it was increasingly futile. "This project will never get done on time unless I do most of the work." As she looked around the table, she realized a couple of others, who always took more than their share of the work, felt the same way. At that moment the door opened and a group member entered the room, 15 minutes late for the meeting.

Sarah took a deep breath and searched for something to give her a handle on how to get this group back on track. She knew that everyone was feeling the time pressure, both to get their project completed and to stay on top of the many other commitments each was facing. Remembering the concept of boundaries, she could see that the group had not adequately defined the *working role boundary*. Tasks had not been systematically assigned. People just picked up what interested them. Sarah realized that she and other group members were going to have to push the *belief boundary*. They did not believe it was possible for the group to be successful. That would have to change. In addition, given everyone's time pressure, they would have to honor the *time boundary*.

Managing boundaries well can be like getting a new pair of glasses. The ways in which groups become stuck will come into focus. With the new, clearer view, groups can find their way out of what had seemed hopelessly confusing and frustrating situations.

Overview of four types of boundaries

Boundaries affecting groups and teams can take many forms. Each acts as a limit in some way. We have grouped these boundaries into four main types: *boundaries between individuals, how to work together boundaries, elements of work boundaries,* and *imposed boundaries.*

Most people understand **boundaries between individuals.** These boundaries are most often consciously considered. This category describes the impact of how individuals experience each other. The foundation of any group's activities is the interaction between individual group members. The limits of what is acceptable or expected form a number of boundaries. Generally, a group operates most effectively when these boundaries between individuals are honored by its members.

For individuals to be effective as a group, they must agree on the **how to work together boundaries**. These boundaries include those concerning how the group completes units of work, uses resources, and assigns accountability for tasks. Not discussing these boundaries and assuming they already are known and held in agreement literally traps a group. Getting caught in these traps leads to conflict, confusion, and failure to complete work. In our experience as consultants and facilitators, adequately addressing these boundaries represents the biggest opportunity for quality and productivity improvements for most groups and organizations.

To be productive, teams must challenge what they believe to be true, expand what they know, change their behaviors, and respond differently emotionally. These are referred to as the **elements of work boundaries**. Thinking of them as boundaries enables a group to determine where they wish to reposition particular boundaries, as well as identify specific, concrete approaches and tools they can use to push them.

Groups do not operate in vacuums with unlimited resources to accomplish whatever they choose. There are limits established by others, the **imposed boundaries**. Some of these limits are set consciously, such as the work that is to be done and the resources made available. Other boundaries, such as organizational policies, laws, and ethics, exist more in the background and are only occasionally considered. Failure to honor these imposed boundaries can result in serious sanctions against group members and/or the group as a whole.

Boundaries that impact groups

The number of boundaries that impact the performance of groups is large. Although naming and defining particular boundaries may be a somewhat arbitrary process, ignoring them puts your group at risk. Whatever they are called, however they are distinguished, boundaries affect the performance of groups and teams. Tables 9-1 through 9-4 on the following pages list the wide variety of boundaries to which a skilled facilitator must be willing to dedicate time and energy.

Table 9-1   Boundaries between individuals

Role	This boundary differentiates among the roles of group member, facilitator, and counselor. Each has distinct responsibilities, opportunities, and pitfalls.
Intellectual	Groups and individuals must have space to think, speak, and make decisions for themselves.
Emotional	Groups and individuals must have space to experience their emotions and express them in appropriate ways.
Space	To feel comfortable, individuals must have a buffer of space around them. Groups and individuals have a space beyond this buffer within which they experience being included and engaged. Beyond this limit, individuals can feel excluded or disengaged.
Physical	Individuals have differing limits on the nature and extent of actual physical contact they allow between themselves and others. Some violations of this boundary can lead to sexual harassment charges.
Sexual	Although individuals may have differing limits regarding expressions of attraction/sexual interest or distribution or viewing of materials of a sexual nature, the changing legal environment has made this the most widely identified boundary.
Privacy	Personal information shared in confidence, either during a group meeting or at another time, is expected to remain in confidence and not be shared.
Property	Individuals and groups experience limits in the use by others of their personal and work-related property.
Time	Individuals and groups experience limits in how their time is valued. Examples of how this valuing can be experienced include attendance, punctuality, and attention.

Table 9-2 Boundaries affecting how to work together

Ground rules	Ground rules are basic agreements among group members regarding how they expect to interact with each other. These are self-imposed limits on behavior.
Work processes	Each group's agreements include how members will work together, including how they make decisions and resolve conflicts. These constraints can help focus a group on accomplishing its task.
Working roles	A key part of working together is assigning one-time or repeated tasks to particular individuals or subgroups. To be effective, a group needs its individuals to understand what is expected of them.
Use of resources	This boundary describes how the group allocates resources within the group to complete its work. It describes what resources are or are not available to particular individuals or subgroups.

Table 9-3   Boundaries defining elements of the work

What is known	There is a limit to what is known at any particular time. Groups have a collective knowledge base about the organization, the work, and how they have worked together in the past. This boundary must often be pushed in order to complete the assigned task.
Beliefs	This boundary describes what is believed to be real or true. Only what is within this boundary can be trusted and acted on with confidence. Beliefs are often expressed in the form of assumptions.
Behaviors	Individuals and groups establish patterns of behaviors. The more established, the more firmly the patterns act as limits on future behaviors. This boundary must often be pushed in order to complete assigned tasks.
Emotional responses	Individuals and groups establish patterns of how they respond emotionally to particular events. The more firmly established patterns act as limits on future behaviors. This boundary must often be pushed in order to complete assigned tasks.
Interdependence	Individuals and groups identify others whose cooperation and/or collaboration is required in order for both to complete assigned tasks. This interdependent relationship creates limits on their interactions. These limits reinforce the relationship.
Us vs. them	Individuals and groups also identify others as having different interests. In a highly competitive environment, this boundary may be defined within a group, between groups, or between departments, divisions, or other corporate designations. It is not limited to "our company vs. the competition."

Table 9-4   Boundaries that are imposed

Charge to group	This boundary describes the expectations of those who establish and/or sanction the group. It defines the assigned tasks that must be accomplished for the group to be a success.
Nature of tasks	Characteristics of tasks, such as their size, complexity, skills and knowledge required, and time limits all define this boundary.
Resources available	A group is bound by the resources it has available to complete a task. These resources include people (number, skills, knowledge, experience, personalities, and so on), technology, time, and money.
Delegated authority	Groups require a variety of authorities to operate and fulfill their Charge. Authority can include the right to meet, take action, use resources, and expect others to act upon request. Sufficient authority to complete a task may or may not accompany a Charge. Groups must decide how to proceed successfully.
Organizational policies	Organizations have formal, written or verbal policies that define what is expressly allowed and prohibited within the organization. These policies may appear to be uniformly, randomly, or never enforced.
Organizational politics	Power in organizations is often exercised as much informally as formally. A whole set of expectations and limits can arise from the informal exercise of power. These boundaries may coincide or be in conflict with the organization's mission and policies.
Cultural norms	Cultural norms are expectations of members of particular cultures. Individuals and groups usually operate in an environment with overlapping cultures—for example, a national culture, an organizational culture, and ethnic cultures. Cultural norms provide guidance for what the culture finds acceptable and unacceptable.
Ethical standards	Ethical standards reflect widely accepted views about what is good and bad and tend to be valid across cultural and national groups. Ethical standards are nearly universally upheld as desirable, even by people who violate them. These standards are often codified in the form of well-publicized codes of ethics.

(continued on next page)

Table 9-4 **Boundaries that are imposed** (continued)

Laws and regulations	Governmental laws and regulations create specific limits on individual and group activities and behaviors. Many applicable laws and regulations may not be well known to group members.
Facilitator is short-term or long-term	There is a distinct boundary between what a facilitator can do if working with a group for only a few days as opposed to what can be done if working through the life of a group.
Facilitator is internal or external	A facilitator who comes from outside an organization will have very different perspectives, acceptance, and potential history with a group than a facilitator who comes from within an organization.

Boundaries do not stand in isolation

Boundaries do not exist completely separate from one another, but rather overlap. They are interconnected and serve to integrate the social and technical structure of interpersonal relationships and the organization. Each boundary is a limit. In most situations, more than one boundary limits a group's activities. Altogether these boundaries create a relatively limited area that remains unconstrained (see Figure 9-1). It is within this unconstrained area that groups work.

A group's task must be completed within the limits set by the various boundaries. A group can work only within the existing limits. Sometimes the unconstrained area does not change. At other times, part of the work itself is to rearrange the boundaries in some way. One outcome of this work may be that the unconstrained area is enlarged in the direction of the boundary that has been pushed. An example of this result (see Figure 9-2) begins with a group that determines that its resources for a project are not adequate. The unconstrained space, created by the boundaries, is just too small. The group honors the Charge boundary by not pushing to have the Charge modified. It pushes the resources available boundary, however, by asking that an additional individual be added to the group. The result is that the unconstrained area is increased and the group can complete its work.

Figure 9-1 *Working area for groups*

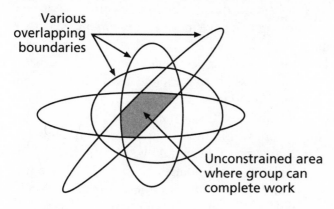

Various overlapping boundaries

Unconstrained area where group can complete work

Figure 9-2 *Revised working area for groups*

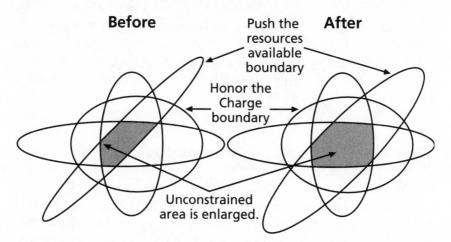

Before Push the resources available boundary **After**

Honor the Charge boundary

Unconstrained area is enlarged.

It is important for a facilitator to understand this fundamental difference in the effect of pushing or honoring boundaries. Initially, it takes more time and effort to push a boundary than to simply work within it. If a boundary should be maintained or does not unduly constrain the work of the group, it is best to work within it. If a boundary significantly hinders or even blocks the success of the group, consideration must be given to pushing it.

It is also important to recognize that the facilitator and his or her group may have a very different perception of critical boundaries than others in the organization, including those issuing the Charge to the group. Pushing a boundary that others believe should be honored may result in the others strongly reasserting the boundary's original position.

Some individuals and groups have more inclination and skill than others in identifying various boundaries. The ability to discern boundaries provides helpful information, especially to someone responsible for facilitating a group. It is possible to complete tasks without a conscious awareness of these boundaries, but it is much more difficult to work efficiently and effectively without that awareness. Every day facilitators and groups work within their unique sets of boundaries. Some of the boundaries are known, even if they are not referred to as boundaries. The vast majority of boundaries, though, which are less consciously identified, nevertheless have an impact on performance. Even without intentional consideration of boundaries, some people possess a strong "natural gift" for helping groups work successfully within their boundaries. This intuitive approach to facilitation can be referred to as the "art of facilitation." Understanding the management of boundaries (as well as other aspects of group dynamics, change processes, systems thinking, tools, and the Facilitation Model) can be referred to as the "science of facilitation." Productive facilitation can take place using primarily either the "art" or the "science." Superior facilitators develop and use both.

Facilitation is boundary management

Managing boundaries is a primary task for facilitators, but one that must be shared with a group. Every boundary impacts the performance of the group. Figure 9-3 depicts the boundary management process. The first stage of boundary management is *awareness*. A facilitator needs to be aware of the many boundaries that exist and consciously choose which ones to raise for discussion. Other boundaries may not need to be discussed unless problems arise with them or the facilitator anticipates a problem. Although group members may not describe them as boundaries, the members can be expected to be aware of a number of them as well.

The second stage is *deciding whether to discuss* a particular boundary. Not all boundaries need to be discussed for a group to be productive. It may be better for the group to get on with completion of its

Figure 9-3 Boundary management process flow

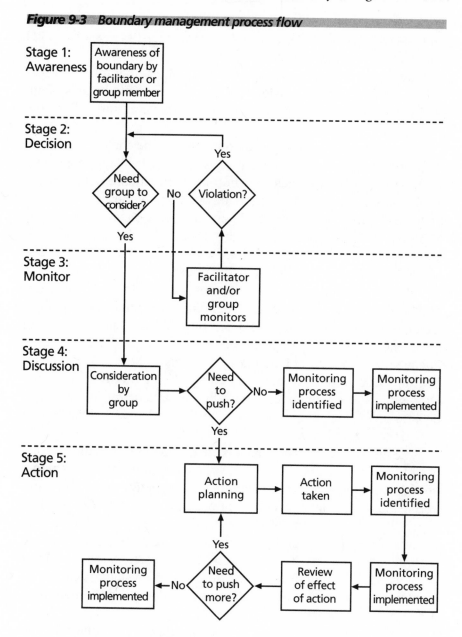

tasks. Skilled facilitators consciously review the various boundaries and make these choices [see Tables 9-5 through 9-14 (pages 162–171) for examples of this process].

Group members also make choices about whether to raise a particular boundary for discussion. They may or may not be as systematic, however, about reviewing the many boundaries and making the choices.

The third and fourth stages are outcomes of the choices made previously. The third stage is a *monitoring* stage. The facilitator and group members have an awareness of a boundary but choose not to raise it for discussion. Instead, they watch the operation of the group for signs that there is a problem with the boundary. Most often, monitoring is appropriate for boundaries that are expected to be honored. This intentional observation helps a group avoid problems by delaying discussion when other work has a higher priority.

The fourth stage, a *discussion* of a boundary by the group, has four possible outcomes: (1) push the boundary, (2) honor it, (3) monitor for possible problems, and (4) a combination of these. Identifying these choices focuses the group's discussion on its choices for productive action. Whether initiated by a facilitator or by a group member, such discussions are an important step in the health of the group. Discussing some boundaries can easily lead to lengthy, unproductive debates unless the group focuses on the practical impact of the boundary on the task at hand.

The fifth stage for managing a particular boundary is the *carrying out of the action* to push it, honor it, and/or monitor it. Pushing a boundary requires thoughtful planning and sensitive execution. Monitoring must begin immediately to provide the feedback required. It is especially helpful when an attempt is made to reinforce the original boundary point. Monitoring may result in a sequence of discussion, planning, action, monitoring, and more discussion. When at least some aspect of a boundary is to be honored, the resulting action may be of two types: (1) action to honor the boundary and (2) monitor to detect boundary violations.

Figure 9-3 depicts how this process flows from one stage to another and sometimes loops back to earlier stages. Upon returning to the discussion stage, different outcomes may result each time because new information is available.

Ten boundaries requiring the most attention

All of the boundaries listed in Tables 9-1 through 9-4 (pages 152–155) should receive attention from a skilled facilitator. Yet, our experience has shown that ten of these boundaries require more attention than the others. These boundaries, which demand attention because they cause problems more frequently or the problems they cause are more serious, include the following:

Boundaries between individuals
- Intellectual
- Sexual
- Privacy

How to work together boundaries
- Work processes
- Working roles
- Use of resources

Elements of the work boundaries
- Beliefs
- Us vs. them

Imposed boundaries
- Charge to group
- Resources available

One of these boundaries, the sexual boundary, has received a lot of attention in recent years. Increasing litigation involving sexual harassment has pushed most organizations to define the sexual boundary in the workplace more clearly. Yet, in our work, we have identified many unique boundaries and know there are more to explore. The sexual boundary is only one of the many boundaries a highly skilled facilitator has to help a group manage.

Tables 9-5 through 9-14 (on the following pages) each examines one of these ten boundaries in detail. The tables are designed to provide a facilitator with an easy reference for both understanding a particular boundary and taking helpful, practical steps to deal with it. Each table includes the following sections: a brief *description* of the boundary, an explanation of *why* it is on the list, its *impact* on a group, how to *clarify* it, whether to *push* it, processes for *monitoring and maintaining* it, the *role of the facilitator* in dealing with it, and appropriate tools from the *tool box* for addressing the boundary. The tools are described in detail in Chapter 8.

Table 9-5 Intellectual boundary

Description	Group and individuals have the time and opportunity to think, speak, and make decisions for themselves.
Why on top 10 list	Not giving group members space to contribute is one of the most common problems for groups. It is a key reason why many groups are less effective. Group members are much less likely to contribute their commitment and their creativity.
Impact	When the boundary is honored, group members can be attentive to their work and accomplish their goals. Ideas are exchanged in a free and easy manner. When conflict arises, it can be dealt with easily. Group members have ownership of outcomes. When the boundary is dishonored, group members cannot focus on completing the tasks necessary to accomplish their goals. Group members feel isolated and have little ownership in group outcomes. Group members do not experience the group as a safe place to express themselves.
Clarifying this boundary?	Select process tools that invite the sharing of ideas and tools that help in collective decision-making support for maintaining this boundary. Develop a contract that addresses the following: • How will conflict be addressed in the group? • How will the group ensure that all voices are heard in discussions? • How will the group make decisions?
Push this boundary?	The intellectual boundary should not be pushed to change. This boundary is an important foundation for the interaction among those in a group.
Monitoring and maintaining	The intellectual boundary should be monitored carefully. This boundary is more difficult to maintain when the facilitator also has other responsibilities such as group leader or manager. Fear of repercussions may inhibit participation by group members.
Role of facilitator	The facilitator, through the activities used, can create space for group members to think, speak, and make decisions for themselves. The facilitator must always be on the alert for violations of this boundary and be willing to address them.
Using the tool box	• Brainstorming • Multi-voting • Consensus

Table 9-6 *Sexual boundary*

Description	It is inappropriate, and generally illegal, for facilitators or group members to: (1) express attraction/sexual interest in group members; (2) refer to the physical appearance of group members; (3) make sexual comments, jokes, or innuendo in discussions; or (4) distribute materials to group members that may be interpreted as sexual in nature, even if distributed outside of group settings. Violations often are identified as sexual harassment.
Why on top 10 list	The current legal environment has created severe criminal penalties for violators and organizations that fail to take appropriate action. Violations also can result in decreases in productivity.
Impact	When this boundary is honored, group members are not concerned about the intrusion and disruption of attraction/sexual interest, references, or materials. They focus on their work and accomplish their goals. When this boundary is crossed, the settings are not experienced as safe by those who are offended. Violation of sexual boundaries can have criminal and civil consequences. Violations result in less productivity by the group.
Clarifying this boundary?	Develop a contract that addresses the following: • How will the group monitor and eliminate expressions of attraction/sexual tension? • How will the group monitor and eliminate all sexual references and materials?
Push this boundary?	Groups should not push for changes in the sexual boundary. This boundary contributes to productivity. There are also legal sanctions for pushing it.
Monitoring and maintaining	The sexual boundary should be monitored carefully. The group must agree to maintain this boundary and be alert for violations. Avoid all comments and materials that could be interpreted as having a sexual nature.
Role of facilitator	Group members often look to the facilitator to gauge what behavior will be allowed. Some may test the boundary in the group setting. Facilitators must monitor this boundary and be willing to address violations. Facilitators need to be aware of corporate guidelines and follow them, as required.
Using the tool box	• Brainstorming • Consensus

Table 9-7 Privacy boundary

Description	Privacy issues pertain to what can be shared in the group and what of group interactions and personal information can be shared with non–group members. Privacy can also pertain to information one group member shares with another but does not want to share with the whole group. In a practical way, this protection comes from the limits contracted within the group. Sharing of some personal information is necessary for a group to function effectively.
Why on top 10 list	Effectively working as a group requires trust. One of the most common ways trust is broken is the inappropriate sharing of information outside of the group context.
Impact	When the boundary is honored, group members are comfortable and are not concerned about whether other group members have talked, outside of group, about them or what they have shared in group. Individuals whose privacy has been violated usually have a strong emotional response, feel much less safe in the group, and often share less in the future. They may also have less investment in the common outcome.
Clarifying this boundary?	Discuss this boundary as part of the creation of ground rules. Having a clear agreement regarding what types of information can be shared outside the group is the most effective aid to maintaining this boundary. Develop a contract addressing the following: • What information should be considered confidential and not shared outside the group? • What information can be readily shared outside the group?
Push this boundary?	The privacy boundary should not be pushed to change. This boundary provides an important foundation for interaction among those in a group.
Monitoring and maintaining	The privacy boundary should be monitored carefully although doing so is more difficult because violations usually take place outside the group. Group members take responsibility for its monitoring.
Role of facilitator	Facilitators must initiate privacy discussions. This boundary can be integrated into the ground rules. Facilitators must always be on the alert for violations of this boundary and be willing to address them.
Using the tool box	• Brainstorming • Consensus

Table 9-8 Work processes boundary

Description	Each group must determine how it will work together to fulfill its Charge. These work processes become limits on how the group operates. They describe what steps and activities will occur and, by default, what steps and activities will not be used.
Why on top 10 list	One of the most common problems is a failure to define work processes. Such a failure seriously undermines the effectiveness and efficiency of a group.
Impact	Failure to define this boundary results in a series of serious and minor breakdowns in productivity. Groups and group members *assume* that everyone knows how to get the work done and that everyone has the same understanding. This is rarely true unless discussed. Without this discussion, groups are creating or recreating their work process. Individuals often use conflicting processes. The group is not focused. Groups with clearly identified work processes act more efficiently and effectively.
Clarifying this boundary?	Creating an acceptable set of work processes requires that the group discuss them prior to beginning the actual work. This is difficult for many groups because they wish to jump right into the work, assuming everyone already knows the processes and has the same view as they do. If true, the task is an easy activity. If not true, significant discussion may be required. Be alert to defining the work process in sufficient detail to be meaningful.
Push this boundary?	Groups that do not currently have effective work processes need to be pushed into developing them.
Monitoring and maintaining	Groups may wish to have periodic review points where they return to the discussion about work processes and evaluate how they are working. Have agreed upon processes not been used? Have other processes been used instead? Alterations in the common work processes may be made.
Role of facilitator	Facilitators are often the only individuals to raise this issue. They must be firm in slowing a group down long enough to discuss its processes. Once the group is at work, the facilitator's role is to help the group use its work processes effectively and efficiently. A key role for facilitators then is to monitor this boundary.
Using the tool box	• Brainstorming • Force field analysis • Cause-effect diagram • Multi-voting • Consensus • Process mapping

Table 9-9   *Working roles boundary*

Description	The working roles boundary is related closely to the group's work processes. Individuals must play roles that ensure that the processes are successful. These roles establish limits for the various group members. Roles may arise from positions held by group members (e.g., group leader or specialist in a functional area), or they may result from more personal attributes (e.g., experience in the field or with the organization, training, personality styles, and interests).
Why on top 10 list	Assumptions about who is to do what usually prove to be invalid unless there has been prior agreement. Without sufficient discussion on this topic, groups can experience serious trouble—work not getting done or done poorly—when the roles are not clear.
Impact	Groups operate more efficiently when they are clear on who is to take particular roles. Individuals can act more decisively when they know what is expected of them. The limits provided by roles allow people to act with the assurance of group approval. When not clarified, roles may overlap and/or have significant gaps. Conflicts and other roadblocks to productivity can arise when unspoken expectations are not met.
Clarifying this boundary?	Groups need to take the time to discuss the various roles that are needed to work the processes they have created. These discussions are an appropriate time to talk about the specific responsibilities of each role, the authority to act within the role, and how the role will be accountable to the whole group.
Push this boundary?	Groups that do not currently have effective processes for matching people and roles need to be pushed into developing them.
Monitoring and maintaining	Group members must be responsible for monitoring their own performance in their roles. They must report what is going well and where there are problems. The rest of the group must perform a secondary level of monitoring by being aware of and responding to those who perform their roles well as well as to those who do not.
Role of facilitator	Facilitators can integrate a discussion of roles with the discussion of work processes and ensure a summary discussion and agreement about roles after the work processes are set. Facilitators can then monitor how the group follows its roles.
Using the tool box	• Brainstorming • Multi-voting • Consensus • Process mapping

Table 9-10 *Use of resources boundary*

Description	Each group has resources available to it that can be used for the successful completion of its Charge. (See Table 9-14.) The group allocates these resources to complete specific tasks. Such an allocation is a boundary that creates limits for individuals and subgroups.
Why on top 10 list	Resources are usually considered to be scarce. Unless this boundary is dealt with, there may be problems with group members and subgroups fighting over resources they feel they need to complete their work.
Impact	Clearly allocating available resources allows the group to use its resources effectively and efficiently. Without creating this boundary, there is likely to be uncertainty about what resources can be used for each specific task, and individuals in the group may compete for resources. Because resource availability is often a sensitive subject for groups, this boundary can reduce unproductive conflict.
Clarifying this boundary?	Clarifying this boundary requires discussion about the priorities that arise from the Charge and Charter. Available resources must be clearly identified and then a frank discussion had about how best to use them. This allocation is included in the group's action plan.
Push this boundary?	Groups that do not currently have effective processes for determining how to allocate resources need to be pushed into developing them.
Monitoring maintaining	Group members need to monitor their own use of resources. If additional resources are required, individuals and subgroups need to return to the full group for renegotiation of either the resources available to them or the task they are to complete.
Role of facilitator	Facilitators often need to initiate a systematic discussion about resources because otherwise the discussion is likely to be only partially completed as parts relate to other issues or conflict arises. The facilitator can structure the discussion to lead to the most helpful outcome and also can be alert to situations where conflicts over resources affect group effectiveness. Facilitators can then monitor this boundary and be willing to address problems and successes.
Using the tool box	• Brainstorming • Consensus • Force field analysis • Multi-voting • Process mapping

Table 9-11   Beliefs boundary

Description	The beliefs boundary describes what is believed to be real or true. Only what is within the boundary can be trusted and acted on with confidence. Beliefs are often expressed as assumptions. People can only commit to what they believe in.
Why on top 10 list	There is no more significant limit than what individuals and groups believe to be real and true. Their beliefs create the reality in which they work.
Impact	Groups cannot seriously address anything outside this boundary. Individuals and groups evaluate their experiences and other information received in light of their beliefs. If the experiences or information is not consistent with what they believe, they will dismiss them or consider them skeptically. Groups frequently fail to deal with realities because they do not believe them to be true.
Clarifying this boundary?	Beliefs are seldom discussed directly because they are taken for granted. People often assume that others believe the same so there is no need to talk about it. Because beliefs are often expressed as assumptions, it is often helpful to initiate discussions about beliefs by generating assumptions. Once beliefs are identified, they can be explored in detail and tested for validity.
Push this boundary?	Often the best solutions are beyond the current reality of a group. By modifying beliefs, additional activities and outcomes can be identified. Beliefs are based on facts, experience, observation of others, and teaching by others. Different people may come to the same beliefs by different paths. When pushing beliefs, it is best to do so openly and with the group's consent.
Monitoring and maintaining	Group members are expected to support the basic beliefs they hold in common. It is easier to monitor this boundary if there is already agreement as to how group members expect to honor them. Group members must be receptive to hearing challenges to their beliefs.
Role of facilitator	Facilitators can help groups identify their individual and collective beliefs in ways that gain maximum participation. Facilitators also have the perspective to notice where beliefs are hindering the group.
Using the tool box	• Brainstorming • Cause-effect diagram • Consensus	• Force field analysis • Multi-voting • Process mapping

Table 9-12 Us vs. them boundary

Description	The us vs. them boundary represents the limit of who is considered to have shared interests in particular outcomes. Personal and organizational history, personal circumstances, and personality styles play key roles in these determinations. The boundary may range from being clearly identified to being permeable.
Why on top 10 list	In highly competitive environments where internal units (e.g., divisions, departments, teams) are pitted against one another, this boundary is readily and firmly defined. It is a distinct roadblock to a group working collaboratively with others.
Impact	In many ways, this boundary defines who is included and who is excluded. People viewed as having shared interests in particular outcomes are experienced as allies. Others are considered either as neutral, at best, or adversaries, at worst. People resist asking for assistance from people who are outside this boundary, the "them's."
Clarifying this boundary?	This boundary can be identified in conjunction with discussions about the Charge to the group and work processes boundaries. Who is seen as allies in their fulfilling their Charge? Talking about this openly is helpful to getting the group's work done.
Push this boundary?	Pushing this boundary occurs in two ways. First, push the boundary out further so more people are considered to be included. Second, make the boundary less distinct, more permeable. Including more people creates opportunities to access additional resources in the effort to achieve desired outcomes. Making boundaries less distinct and more permeable also creates opportunities to utilize additional resources.
Monitoring and maintaining	Periodic examination of how group members are collaborating with each other and with others is a productive way to monitor this boundary. By making such examinations a standard work process, no one need feel targeted by the inquiry. Significant collaboration problems can be dealt with immediately.
Role of facilitator	Facilitators can initiate the first discussion on this topic and help the group explore its current patterns and decide if changes are desired. Facilitators also have the perspective to notice where insufficient collaboration is hindering the group.
Using the tool box	• Brainstorming • Consensus

Table 9-13 *Charge to group boundary*

Description	The Charge consists of the expectations of those who establish and/or sanction the group. The Charge describes the work that is to be done. Anything outside the Charge is beyond the scope of the group. By focusing the work of the group, the Charge limits it, too.
Why on top 10 list	With surprising frequency, groups are not given a clear Charge and/or they do not take the time to understand it. They assume they know what they are supposed to do and immediately begin working, possibly on the wrong work.
Impact	This boundary is a guide for the group regarding what is appropriate activity and what is inappropriate. The consequences for violation of the boundary may range from serious career implications to corrective guidance to nothing.
Clarifying this boundary?	Ask the group about the meaning it makes of its Charge. Asking questions of the establishing party can lead to a clearer Charge and a more productive group. All group members need to be focused on the group's Charge.
Push this boundary?	The primary opportunity to push this boundary arises when a group receives its Charge. After reviewing its resources, a group may wish to negotiate the Charge with those who issued it. If new information indicates that the Charge is no longer viable, then the person issuing the Charge must be contacted for an update.
Monitoring and maintaining	The Charge boundary is most consciously addressed at the time the Charter is developed. Everyone has a responsibility to watch for alignment of activities with the Charge. Periodically, the group should examine its progress in fulfilling its Charge, unless circumstances change significantly. If circumstances do change, then the Charge may have to be changed.
Role of facilitator	The facilitator has a responsibility to help the group gain and maintain clarity on its Charge. The facilitator highlights the importance of this task and provides a process for evaluating the Charge. The facilitator must gauge whether or not the group experiences the Charge as clear, compelling, and attainable. Once the Charge is usable, the facilitator helps group members respond to it with their own Charter.
Using the tool box	• Brainstorming • Consensus

Table 9-14 Resources available boundary

Description	Groups require resources to fulfill their Charge. These resources include people (number, skills, knowledge, experience, personalities, and so on), delegated authority, technology, time, and money. The quantity of resources has a finite limit that can be considered a boundary. (See Table 9-10.)
Why on top 10 list	Nearly every group perceives that it has not been given sufficient resources to satisfactorily complete its work. Frequently a key resource, time, is wasted complaining about the lack of resources.
Impact	Availability of resources clearly affects what courses of action are viable and even when tasks can be completed. Groups commonly debate what is a reasonable amount of work to be produced with given resources.
Clarifying this boundary?	When group members receive a Charge, they should thoroughly inventory their resources. This task is rarely done. Even when they do some form of inventory, groups are rarely systematic about it. In addition to the more usual budgets and group rosters, activities can include skill, personality, and experience inventories to assess personal resources.
Push this boundary?	If there seem to be insufficient resources to fulfill the Charge, then negotiation for additional resources may be required. The best time to negotiate resources is when the Charge is given. If resources are later deemed inadequate to fulfill the Charge, they may need to be renegotiated.
Monitoring and maintaining	Organizations are often quite proficient in monitoring the use of tangible resources, especially money. They are often less proficient in monitoring the use of less tangible resources, such as skills, knowledge, experience, and personalities. Groups must be intentional in performing this task.
Role of facilitator	Groups often rush into "getting on with the work." The facilitator can play a key role in helping a group manage this boundary by creating opportunities to both inventory available resources and monitor their use. The facilitator should have a perspective that helps the group overcome its desire to avoid such activities.
Using the tool box	• Consensus

Improving your facilitation through boundary management

A key aspect of successful facilitation is knowing about the many boundaries that exist in organizations. Because there are so many boundaries, being able to address all of them may seem out of reach. We suggest starting with the ten most problematic boundaries and become proficient with them. But do not try to tackle them all at once. Pick one and help a group be aware of its existence and impact. Then, using the boundary management process described in Figure 9-3, help the group work through some of the other boundaries that have caused problems.

The approach suggested in Tables 9-5 through 9-14 concerning the ten boundaries provides a systematic way for a facilitator to address many of the dynamics within groups that block or hinder their success. Understanding boundaries provides a lens that clarifies the facilitator's view of the actions of group members, the work of the groups, and their work environment.

Facilitation Is Change Management

In this chapter you will learn:

- Different ways people experience change
- A basic unit of change
- Stages of change
- About change as a cascade
- About intervening in change processes
- About the Change Adoption Curve
- How to deal with *resistance* to change

Change. People often react emotionally to the word *change*. Some people feel excitement. Many others feel sadness, anxiety, even fear. Groups are inundated by changes in their organizations and by changes they create themselves. Facilitators must be prepared to deal with their own reactions to change as well as with those of the groups they are helping. If people cannot deal effectively with change, they are going to be much less successful. You can probably think of several examples of individuals, groups, and entire organizations that were not able to anticipate, respond to, and create change. Those were often painful experiences.

We assume you know all about the ways in which change is increasing. We know that *facilitators must play a lead role in helping groups successfully anticipate, respond to, and create change.* Facilitators must understand the nature of change processes, how group members may be experiencing particular changes, and how changes impact the work of a group. The material in this chapter provides facilitators with some practical tools for doing these things.

Responding to change

Change is rarely considered neutral. People almost always have strong feelings about change. We have heard these feelings described as apprehensive, happy, confusing, angry, relieved, hopeful, energetic, and, very often, fearful. Effective facilitators recognize these feelings and support their expression. Facilitators find ways for groups to deal with their strong feelings about change even if the group believes "any expression of feelings is not appropriate in our workplace." Safely addressing these feelings helps such groups be more productive.

Past experiences with change affect how people respond to new changes. There is often a potent history that perhaps includes a major company reorganization, a promotion that created many wonderful opportunities, a layoff that caused hardship to a whole family, a new significant relationship, or the birth of a child. The same change can feel like an opportunity to one person and a disaster to another.

What is change?

The first challenge for a facilitator in dealing with change is to know what it is. Dictionaries provide a range of definitions, including (1) to make or cause something to be different and (2) to make something very different, to transform. Everyone makes little adjustments each day that he or she may not even notice. Often people notice only the accumulation of these little adjustments. For example, compare family photographs taken a year or two apart. Notice how different everyone looks. You may not have noticed the changes day by day, but the differences from year to year may make you laugh or cry.

This accumulation of adjustments happens in the workplace too, but it is rarely called change. Such adjustments are simply brushed off as part of living and working. Instead, most people think of "change" as bigger, turn-my-world-upside-down types of things. Those are the changes that demand a lot of attention. Individuals are forced to make many personal adjustments in response to these larger changes. Revolutionary or transformational changes evoke strong feelings. This continuum of change is described in Figure 10-1.

Many variations of change fall along the continuum presented in Figure 10-1. People who name only the revolutionary or transforming

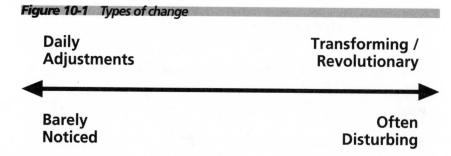

Figure 10-1 *Types of change*

Daily Adjustments

Transforming / Revolutionary

Barely Noticed

Often Disturbing

types of change as "change," do not recognize their own daily experience and ability to successfully deal with change. This experience is a resource to individuals and to groups.

Facilitators can help individuals and groups recognize their expertise with change. Facilitators can call on this experience when individuals or groups feel incapable of successfully dealing with changes. Facilitators must recognize that individuals and groups may not be nearly as inexperienced as they perceive or present themselves.

A basic unit of change

For all human systems, change occurs through a certain fundamental process. This is true whether the human system is an individual or an organization, whether the change is a minor adjustment or a revolutionary transformation. Because change is a process, it is not instantaneous. Analysis of many different types of changes reveals a basic unit to this change process.

At all times, people experience reasons to do something differently **(forces for change)** as well as reasons to keep doing it the same way **(forces for stability)**. An example of a force for change might be hearing from customers that want a product delivered in a new way. A force for stability in this situation might be that other customers say they like the product the old way. Whether consciously or not, we evaluate these forces. We gauge the relative strength of each one. We then seek **a balance point** where these forces offset each other. Current behavior reflects this balance point. In Figure 10-2, each of the arrows represents a particular force. The length of the arrows reflects the relative strength experienced for each force.

Figure 10-2   *Forces for change and forces for stability create a balance point*

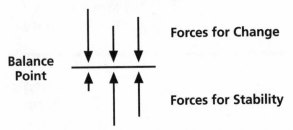

Figure 10-3   *Increase in a force for change*

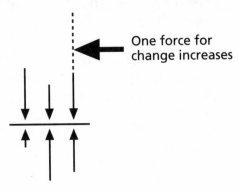

If one or more of the forces for change increase (for example, a department manager states that a particular company policy has changed), the situation is no longer in balance (see Figure 10-3). However, people want to be in balance and will respond as necessary to return to that state.

To regain this balance, we have two ways of responding: (1) increase our assessment of the forces for stability to counter the increase in the forces for change (for example, remind myself that this manager has made such statements before and nothing ever came of them) or (2) adjust our behavior and/or beliefs (for example, make the change and adopt the new work process) to create a new balance point. This whole process is summarized in Figure 10-4.

Once a change is made, some of the old forces for change (for example, the manager's expectation of new behavior) now support maintaining the new work process, and therefore can now be considered forces for stability. Some of the old forces for stability (for example, comfort with and successes gained through the old process) may become forces for change. If the manager turns his or her attention to other demands and no longer is actively supporting the new behavior,

Figure 10-4 *Response choices to an increase in a force for change*

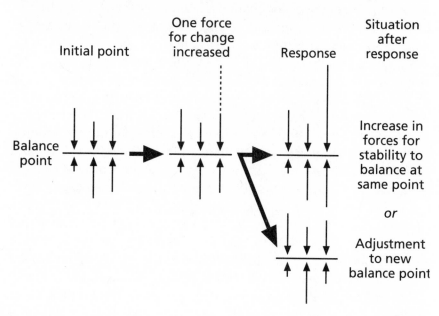

the effect may be a reduction in a force for stability. The system goes out of balance again and, most likely, the person expected to maintain the new behavior makes another adjustment to go back to the old behavior. Many managers have experienced this **rubber-band effect** on changes they thought were adopted. They are at a loss to understand what happened and may even assume the cause was insubordination. However, rather than being a conscious effort to thwart the manager, such behavior is a normal response to the dynamic effects of the forces for change and forces for stability.

Facilitators and groups can often avoid this rubber-band effect by attending to the forces for change and forces for stability. Facilitators help individuals and groups deal with this by identifying the various forces and taking appropriate action. In most cases, *when making a change, it is most effective to focus attention on reducing the forces for stability* (the forces supporting the current behaviors). This is contrary to the usual process of focusing on the forces for change (what can be done to increase the pressure on people to make the change). *By focusing attention on reducing the forces for stability, a group can reduce the probability of returning to the previous behaviors.*

Facilitators have a responsibility to help their groups identify these forces. Although forces for change are usually easy to recognize (for example, a new procedure is announced, expenses are over budget, or a key group member is transferred away from the group), the forces for stability are usually harder to identify. Some, such as past successes using current procedures or lack of resources, are more apparent, but most are less visible because they are taken for granted. We don't think much about gravity, but it keeps us from floating away. We may exert extra effort to jump into the air, but we soon return to the ground. Forces for stability are often embedded in our culture, values, and assumptions. The phrase, "that's not the way we do it around here," is an expression of a force for stability. Simple inertia is also often a powerful force for stability, especially in organizations with long histories of doing things the same way. It takes a lot of energy to overcome that inertia. When people need to make changes, either within the group or within the larger organization, *facilitators can play a key role in helping the groups identify the forces for stability that affect the decisions.* Facilitators can do this by encouraging their groups to expand their list of forces beyond what immediately comes to mind. The elements of a paradigm as discussed in Chapter 5 (behaviors/activities, vocabulary, assumptions/beliefs, and values) help groups discover powerful forces for stability that might otherwise go undetected.

Of critical importance in these processes is how the various forces are evaluated. Identifying the forces is only the first step. Some forces are very influential, whereas others have little impact on current or future behaviors. Assessing the strength of each force, therefore, is critical in understanding a particular change process. Each person or group evaluates a force in its own way because each is using somewhat different criteria. Remember the example of the manager who directed the department to use a new procedure. Some people might make the change immediately because they believe the manager to be serious about the change. Others might ignore the requested change, believing that the manager's interest in it will be short-lived.

The most influential aspect of evaluations is the criteria used to make them. The criteria determine the significance of the forces for change and forces for stability. The 80–20 Rule can be applied here. Twenty percent of the forces have 80% of the effect. Facilitators and groups benefit from knowing which forces have the most influence on current and future behavior, the balance points, and modifying them as necessary. Often, it is in modifying these criteria that the outcome

Table 10-1 *Examples of criteria for evaluating forces for change and forces for stability*

Example of a change being evaluated	Use a new procedure within the department
Forces for Change	**Possible Evaluation Criteria**
Department manager issues directive	• How much do I respect the manager? • How serious do I believe the manager to be about this directive? • How serious would the consequences be if I ignore the directive?
Customer requests change	• How much will this help me better meet the customer's needs? • How do I rate this against other customer requests?
New skills needed for procedure prepares me for other jobs	• Would I like to learn these new skills? • What other jobs will they prepare me for?
This could make my job easier	• How much would it make my job easier? • How hard is the rest of my job? Am I looking for some relief?
Forces for Stability	**Possible Evaluation Criteria**
This is not the way we have done it around here	• How important to me is the procedure that is to be replaced? • How much do I like things the same each day? • How important is this to my being able to continue acting as in the past?
One of my performance standards is based on the old procedure	• How well was I doing on that standard? • What might be substituted?
New skills are required to perform the new procedure	• How much effort do I think it will take to learn the new skills? • How much do I dislike feeling less competent as I learn the new skills?

can be altered. Effectively modifying the criteria can mean much less attention needs to be paid to modifying the actual forces. Table 10-1 provides examples of criteria that might be applied to a change in departmental procedures.

Stages of change

The change process has been described in terms of three to nine stages. We believe a simple three-stage model provides useful information for facilitators. Kurt Lewin, William Bridges, and others have explored this process. Each stage has definite tasks that need to be finished in order for an individual to successfully complete that stage. We have found that all changes create loss, whatever is changed. If the change is significant enough that we are aware of the loss, we have to let go of what used to be before we can move on. This is the **Good-bye** stage, where individuals must grieve and release the old. Once the grieving is over, everyone must face the learning curve associated with the new. This is the **Muddling** stage, an often difficult stage to navigate. Everyone must go from being the expert to being a learner. The task of this stage is to learn the basic information needed for what is new, practice using it, and gain some confidence in it. Only after successfully navigating the Muddling stage can people begin to really embrace the changes, even become excited about them. This last stage is called **Hello**. It continues until the new way is taken for granted. This stage requires perfecting the new, experiencing some successes, and feeling at ease enough to turn attention elsewhere. It is in the Hello stage, more than the Muddling stage, that a person understands the change well enough to suggest and/or make improvements to it.

People experience these stages differently and pass through them at different speeds. These differences are the result of how they evaluate the change. Good-bye and Muddling cannot be skipped.

For each stage, certain tasks must be completed. Unfinished tasks will resurface openly or covertly. The Hello stage is often seen as the desired state, but at this stage as well there are tasks to be completed. All three stages must be completed before change takes hold. Tables 10-2 through 10-4 summarize the nature of each stage and the work that needs to be completed before we can pass out of the stage.

Table 10-2 Good-bye stage	
General Observations	• Every change must begin with letting go of something—every change involves loss. • It is a time when the success of the past is questioned—why else would there be a change now? • We tend to focus on the past, reviewing what happened and how we felt about it.
Emotional Experience	• The initial emotional experience may be shock, which can temporarily immobilize us. • We tend to look to what was and feel sadness and loss. • We often experience at least some fear; maybe we won't be successful using what is new. • We may consider quitting or other ways of not caring so much about the way things are.
Work Performance	• Work performance is reduced due to reallocation of energy to deal with loss. • Work performance is reduced because we continue to use the old (e.g., approach, system, and so on) after others have changed.
Stage Task	• Grieve the loss of what was. • Release doing/being the old way.
What Can Be Done to Help	• Celebrate the old way to acknowledge how well it worked under the old conditions. • Support people's grieving while being clear that the old way has ended.

Impact of overlapping stages

Different people enter the stages of change at different times. Some complete a given stage faster or slower than others. Also, the time that people take to complete the three steps varies from change to change. Each person views a specific change from the perspective of the stage she or he is in at that moment.

In the illustration in Figure 10-5 (page 183), three people are responding to the same change. Person A starts the process in Good-bye and may share that perspective with person B for a short time. Once person A enters Muddling, that shared perspective ends and the two people experience the change very differently. By the time person C enters the Good-bye stage, person A has entered Hello and person B

Table 10-3   Muddling stage

General Observations	• This is that awkward time after we let go of what was but have not yet embraced what will be.
	• It is a painful period when we no longer know how to do things as well as we did before.
	• We tend to focus on the present; we are struggling too much to climb the learning curve to think much about the future.
Emotional Experience	• Our self-confidence is at its lowest. We have jumped from being an expert in the old way to a novice in the new way.
	• Being at the bottom of the learning curve doesn't feel good.
Work Performance	• Work performance dips to the lowest point due to lack of knowledge and experience with the new.
	• Work performance also suffers because of the emotional price being paid during this stage.
Stage Task	• Learn the basic information needed for the new.
	• Create experiences with the new.
	• Gain confidence.
What Can Be Done to Help	• Understand the uncertainty people are experiencing.
	• Provide information about succeeding using the new way .
	• Provide encouragement and tell people they can be successful again.

is in Muddling. They do not share much of a common perspective on this particular change. Person A is now focused on the future, perfecting the ways to be successful, believing in the positive aspects of the change. Person B is in the last stages of learning the new way and gaining confidence. Person C is focused on the past, still grieving about what is being lost.

Often person A was part of the management group that participated in planning the change, whereas persons B and C learn of the changes later. Too many times, persons A and B have management or supervisory responsibility for person C. In many cases, person C is the one experiencing the most change and losing the most. He or she has more to say good-bye to. If the managers do not understand these

Table 10-4 Hello stage

General Observations	• Competency is achieved in fits and starts as more is learned and experienced. • We have more focus on the future when we believe things will be even better.
Emotional Experience	• There is hope. • We feel more confident in our ability to be successful. • Enthusiasm for the change can be felt for the first time. • The emotional "high" fades as the new becomes routine.
Work Performance	• We begin to catch on. • Performance finally rises above the level previously achieved under the old way.
Stage Task	• Perfect using/acting the new way. • Experience successes with the new way. • Focus attention increasingly on other changes or tasks.
What Can Be Done to Help	• Encourage people's enthusiasm. • Continue to provide information about how to be successful. • Recognize people's successes.

Figure 10-5 Overlapping stages

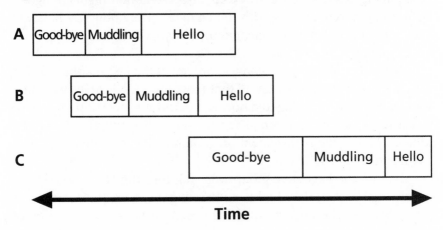

stages of change, they can develop a negative opinion of person C, who is only conscientiously trying to complete the tasks in the Good-bye stage.

Figure 10-5 can also be used in a different way. It can depict three different changes (A, B, and C) that one person is experiencing. This person could be in the early part of the Hello stage for change A, in the Muddling stage for change B, and in the Good-bye stage for change C. Think of the vastly different emotions this person is experiencing as a result of dealing with these changes, all at the same time. The fast and furious pace of change in the workplace is creating an emotional roller coaster.

Facilitators can take very practical action (see Tables 10-2 through 10-4) to help people use their emotions as a catalyst for doing the real work associated with each stage of change. They can help group members realize that their feelings about a particular change are normal. Once this level of understanding is achieved, facilitators can encourage the group to work through the stages.

An executive had just told one of her direct reports that he had a new job as a result of a reorganization. The direct report used to be a regional sales manager. He was responsible for a staff of 24 people and a territory covering seven states. His new title was group leader and his new staff consisted of a cross-functional group of eight people. He was expected to act more as a facilitator than a territorial manager in order to help his group be more responsive to customers. He was told that the annual sales retreat, scheduled for the following week, would be a training session for new group leaders.

At the kickoff of the training session, the executive group in charge of the reorganization gave an excellent presentation highlighting the benefits that were coming with the changes. They honestly believed they were doing something great and encouraged the new group leaders to join in.

When the former sales manager arrived at the first training session for new group leaders, he found that most of his colleagues were in a bad mood. "We are being told how wonderful this new opportunity is, but it feels like a demotion. The sales incentive program has been eliminated and the replacement program has not yet been developed. I can't believe this!"

Clearly, the executive group was well into the Hello stage—not surprising because they had been working on the reorganization for nine months. The new group leaders were at the very beginning of

Good-bye. Some had learned of their new appointment only the day before the training. They were not ready or even able to benefit much from the training. The individual facilitating this session recognized that they needed to say good-bye to aspects of the organization and their jobs that had meant a lot to them. That became the first order of business.

Facilitators need to be aware of these stages and of the complex inter-actions of multiple changes and personal differences in completing change-related tasks. Using this information, facilitators can help both individuals and groups address the work to be completed in each stage in the most efficient manner. (Look again at the section "What can be done to help" in Tables 10-2 through 10-4.) Naming this work as "real work" is often the most valuable contribution a facilitator can make.

Rituals can help people let go of what was. These rituals recognize the value of what was, how people had been invested in it, and the void they will experience with it gone. Rituals might be as simple as having each person share his or her thoughts and stories about the old way. Or they might be more involved, such as a mock funeral. Such rituals cannot be underestimated as an effective way of saying good-bye.

As group members go through Muddling, facilitators help groups identify information they need to be successful, acknowledging the extent of uncertainty members are experiencing. When groups reach the Hello stage, facilitators help the groups identify their passage through the process and acknowledge their accomplishments.

Change as a cascade

Typical changes in organizations consist of a series of basic units of change being completed by individuals or groups at their own pace. The completion of one person's or group's basic unit often initiates a basic unit of the change process for others. Organizational change can therefore be viewed as a cascading process. For example, a decision by a company's management group to make a significant change does not instantaneously change the whole organization. In reality, it initiates a cascade of changes, with each individual or group responding to changes made by those before them in the cascade. They also are affected by their own earlier changes (see Figure 10-6). The cumulative

Figure 10-6 Cascading nature of change

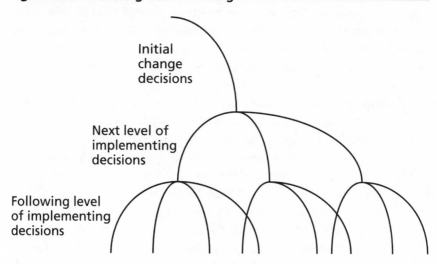

Initial
change
decisions

Next level of
implementing
decisions

Following level
of implementing
decisions

effect of these cascading changes is what is referred to as "organizational change."

It is easy to see why large-scale organizational changes often vary significantly from the intent of those who initiated the process. Each individual and group has its own unique way of making change decisions. Leaders who initiate a change usually have an image of how the organization will operate once the change is complete. For large-scale organizational changes, this image is often expressed in a vision statement. However, the actual outcome often varies from this initial image. In Figure 10-6, the width of the cascade at the bottom depicts this variance. If the leaders do a good job of helping the organization develop a shared vision, this variance is less. If the vision is not clear or if people do not have ways of creating a common meaning for it, the resulting change may be far different from what was intended.

Intervening in the change process

Facilitators are often called upon to initiate or support changes. *The information covered in this chapter can help facilitators suggest action steps that can lead to implementing change in more efficient and effective ways*. Although "change agents" often attempt to create change by increasing one or more forces for change, this is not the most effective tactic. In fact, as noted earlier, the change model shows that primary attention should go to decreasing the forces for stability.

Facilitators and groups also can affect change by targeting the criteria used to evaluate the forces for change and forces for stability. Facilitators can help groups explore the criteria they are using, identify additional criteria that might be used, and even discard criteria that are no longer relevant. Being alert to the role these evaluation criteria play in change processes, groups can seek to have an impact on the criteria used elsewhere in their organizations.

An important intervention opportunity for facilitators in group settings is to help people complete the stages of change. Particular attention can be paid to the tasks that must be completed during each stage. Facilitators can create activities that help group members focus needed attention on these tasks and complete them successfully. (See Table 10-5 on page 188 for examples of how and where to intervene in change processes.)

Rank ordering of systems

The rank ordering of systems, first discussed in Chapter 6, can have a significant impact on change processes. This concept describes how people are part of many systems at the same time. Some of these may be subsets of larger systems. Individuals rank the importance of each system to them. A particular system's ranking directly affects how forces for change and forces for stability are evaluated. One of the most common evaluation criteria for forces for change is "How will it affect me?" When people ask this question, they are really asking, "How will this change affect my most important systems?"

If the increase in a force for change affects a highly ranked system, more information usually will be gathered and more evaluation will take place. Forces for change affecting low-ranking systems usually are ignored, screened out to focus more attention on higher-ranking systems. This process helps individuals and groups sift through the immense amount of information flooding over them and deal more effectively with the higher priority areas. However, it also can create serious problems, if they are not careful.

Table 10-5   *Examples of where to intervene in change processes*

Examples of Intervention Areas	Examples of Intervention Activities
Decreasing forces for stability	
• Reward and recognition programs reinforce the old	• Modify reward and recognition programs to reinforce the new.
• People do not currently have skills to do the new	• Make sure people have the opportunity to learn the skills required by the new.
• Taken-for-granted assumptions support the old	• Provide credible information that contributes to new assumptions that support the new.
• Words people use still refer to the old	• Introduce new vocabulary so people can know you are speaking of the new.
• Cultural norms support the old, not the new	• Modify cultural norms so they support the new.
Targeting evaluation criteria	
• How serious is the company about this change?	• Provide information that clarifies how serious the company is about completing this change.
• How would I rate this request against other customer requests?	• Discuss this criterion and clarify how the company evaluates this customer request.
• How will this change affect my ability to succeed in this company?	• Provide information that clarifies how performance will be evaluated in the new.
Complete tasks associated with stages of change	
• People not able to let go of the past	• Hold a ritual such as a "mock funeral."
• People concerned about making mistakes while learning the new	• Reassure them that mistakes are expected and that they are to learn from them—failure will not be punished.
• People isolated in the ways they are going about the new	• Celebrate the successes that come from having learned the new.

The CEO of a large corporation received an e-mail from a group protesting the recent change of the company's name. The group leaders said they had decided not to use the new name because they did not believe it would be successful with their customers. The CEO told the group leaders that he understood the pride and connection the group had with the old name. He made it clear, however, that the change had been adopted by the whole organization and the group could not put its desires above the larger corporation.

If groups are not consciously thinking about how they rank their systems, it is harder for them to be alert to the impact of those rankings on their evaluation of the forces for change and the forces for stability. A facilitator could have helped the group in the preceding example be aware of how their rankings caused them to evaluate a force for change, the announcement of the name change, very differently from what the CEO intended. The response from the CEO made that much clearer.

People adopt change at different times

Although organizational leaders would like everyone to complete a particular change instantaneously, the reality is that people do not change at the same time. They do not even begin the process at the same time or complete the stages simultaneously. Only by coincidence do some people complete a change process at approximately the same time.

Reasons for these differences

There are three primary reasons for this variance in completing a change process.

1. *Each individual must complete the stages of change in his or her own way.* Some may care little about what will change, whereas others may have a deep investment in the way it was. Some may find the new way difficult to adopt whereas others may find it quite easy.
2. *People throughout an organization are not asked at the same time to make a change.* Some positions are more responsible for identifying and leading such changes; others are more insulated.

3. *Each individual and group evaluates the forces for change differently.* Because of this, some may feel a strong sense of urgency to make the change, whereas others find it insignificant.

These reasons also cause people to adopt particular changes at different times.

Three roles in adopting change

The differences in timing of when people adopt a particular change are reflected in the Change Adoption Curve presented in Figure 10-7. The curve is created by identifying the first 16% who adopt the change. They are called the **Initiators**. The next 68% are referred to as the **Majority**. The final 16% are identified as **Defenders**. By definition, every change has Initiators, Majority, and Defenders. If the change is fully adopted quickly within an organization, the horizontal axis of the graph simply reflects less time, but the people in the organization can still be identified as Initiators, Majority, or Defenders for that change.

The Initiators, Majority, and Defenders all have roles to play in the adoption of a particular change, although they probably do not identify with these labels. People may or may not consciously choose these roles, but they do balance each other.

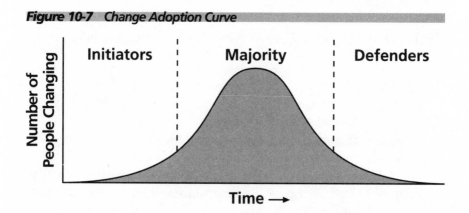

Figure 10-7   Change Adoption Curve

In Western society, the Initiator role is the one most often recognized for its contribution. Boldly creating something new is valued highly, even if it does not work as well as hoped. Initiators are most often seen as the leaders in an organization.

The Majority changes when enough people around them change. They look not only to the information provided by the Initiators, but also to their peers. They want to see evidence that the change has merit. They also want to be reassured that this change is really being accepted.

Defenders are often viewed negatively by those driving the change, but they play an important role for an organization. It is a role that is rarely recognized for its positive impact on the organization. Defenders balance the more impulsive nature of the Initiators with an appreciation for the ways that have worked in the past. They articulate valid concerns that an organization ignores at its peril. They also require more time to complete the change process than nearly everyone else. Once they have adopted the new way, they will be very loyal to it.

Although people have a tendency to play one role, they are not rigidly tied to it. An individual may be an Initiator for one change, a Majority member for another, and a Defender for yet another change. They may prefer to be in one role in one environment, such as work, and a different role in another environment, such as home.

Table 10-6 summarizes the information about these roles.

Table 10-6 Roles for each group involved in adopting change

Initiators	• Create responses to environmental changes • Keep organization current • Look more to the future on this issue
Majority	• Do the bulk of the work in the organization • Are cautious but willing to adjust • Look more to the present
Defenders	• Protect the identity of the organization • Value what has been successful in the past • Challenge the need to change and the specifics of a change

Dealing with "resistance" to a change

In many situations, there are people labeled as "resistors" to change. A few examples are:

- A facilitator suggests a set of process steps to help a group accomplish its task. One or more group members say, "No, we don't want to do it that way!"
- A group has agreed to achieve consensus on a particular decision. Most of the group is in agreement, but a couple of group members say, "We can't live with that choice."
- A group is charged with initiating a change within the larger organization. Significant resources (time and money) have already been spent on this project. As the change is rolled out, a number of people in the organization are very vocal in stating, "This is a bad idea. We should keep doing it the old way."

Conventional wisdom says that these are all examples of resistance to change. Resistant behavior often is framed as a problem, an enemy that must be overcome. One of the most common requests we receive for a *quick fix* is how to effectively deal with resistance. We hear comments like, "These people are not on board! They are undermining our work. How do we get them on board, quickly?"

"Resistor" and "resistance" are such loaded topics. The words *resistor* and *resistance* evoke images of someone actively trying to prevent someone else from accomplishing something. The words evoke images of combat. In nearly every war, there have been *resistance* movements fighting and sabotaging invaders. There are also descriptions of the human body *resisting* the invasion of a dangerous bacteria or virus by attacking it with white blood cells. Thinking of "resistance" in organizations in terms of such a life-or-death struggle leads to viewing the "resistors" as the enemy: dangerous.

Common strategies for reducing "resistance"

Assuming that "resistance" is a problem leads to a number of strategies designed to eliminate it. Each of these strategies can be viewed as heavy-handed or manipulative. If that is the way they are perceived by those on the receiving end, the strategies will backfire, and acceptance of a change will take much longer. Such strategies for dealing with a problem arise from common beliefs about what causes "resistance."

If you believe that "resistors" naturally hate change and are consciously intent on thwarting it, then you probably also believe that this threat should be overcome. One common way to do that is to combat the "resistance" with variations of "tell them to get with the program or find another job." The hope is that this will get the resistors' attention and control them. However, the reality is that this will force them to comply but they will continue to reject the change. This is not a situation conducive to people utilizing a change in the most productive way.

If the source of the "resistance" is assumed to be lack of information rather than just obstinacy, then a form of education strategy might be chosen. "If I only could give them enough of the information I have, they will understand why we need to make this change. Then they will support it." The assumption here is that such choices are logical and the person is missing important information. However, if the source of concern about the change is not lack of information, this approach does not help people accept the change more readily.

A third belief is that people need to experience some control over their own lives, including organizational change, in order to accept changes. This may lead to some form of significant participation but, when "resistance" is anticipated, often it is treated in a much more cavalier way: "Find something or some way they can talk about this, even make a decision or two to create the desired 'buy-in.'" However, insincere use of this strategy breaks down trust within the organization. This approach makes it more difficult to introduce changes later.

Each of these strategies may be effective in gaining the desired behavior changes. We do not disagree that the strategies can be appropriate and useful in helping people adopt some changes. We do believe that these strategies are more likely to be used inappropriately if the terms *resistor* and *resistance* are used. Use of the terms limits the ways change situations are evaluated and options chosen.

Facilitators encounter a wide variety of change situations as they go about their work. Those who wear both the leader and manager hats may be tempted to identify slower than expected acceptance of change as "resistance" and therefore choose less productive, manipulative, or coercive strategies. The outcome may be short-term progress at the expense of longer-term cooperation.

Effects of the "resistor" lens

Calling behavior "resistance" and the individual a "resistor" clicks a lens into place, creating a negative trigger. Behaviors, words, even "a certain look in the eye" now have a ready interpretation. With the high pressure to get more done in less time, it is improbable that a facilitator will, once a reasonable interpretation is available, look further.

The resistance lens involves some basic assumptions that are not true. It assumes a situation in which people must choose either the new or the old. If the person chooses the new behavior, the person initiating the change wins. If the old way is chosen, then the Initiator loses. Facilitators can help groups choose different approaches than this competitive, win–lose approach to change. Using the Conflict Resolution Process (described in Chapter 6; the steps include expression of differences, awareness of conflict, agreement on commonality, clarification of differences, and resolution of conflict), facilitators can help the Initiators and Defenders find common ground and work together on the change.

We have found that these labels are much more likely to be used in organizations that tend toward the adversarial end of the 6C Relationship Model (described in Chapter 5 as a continuum from Coercion to Collaboration). Challenging or passive resistance is more common in Competitive and Coercive types of relationships.

Alternative interpretations

There are several benign reasons for behaviors that might be labeled "resistance." One of the most common is the ways in which people overlap in passing through the stages of change. Figure 10-8 shows a manager well into the Hello stage when she introduces a change into her work group.

In this case, the group immediately enters the Good-bye stage. One of the workers in the group has had a deep investment in the old approach and has a long Good-bye and Muddling stage. The manager has long finished her process and doesn't even think of the approach as new. To her, the behavior of the worker could easily appear to be resistance. The worker is still longing for the old way and is not consistently exhibiting the new behavior. *Treating this as "resistance" is wrong.* Although the worker may need to be reminded that the change

Figure 10-8   Impact of overlapping stages

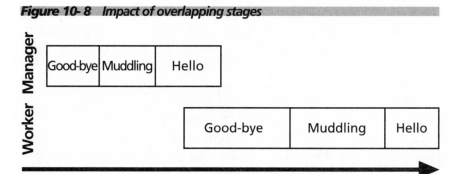

is real and must be adopted, a manager who understands the Good-bye stage can be more helpful. After all, the manager had a head start in completing the change stages. Her *job* is to help the worker complete the tasks associated with that stage (grieve the losses and release the old).

An individual also may be playing the Defender role. People fulfilling this role are often looked at with disdain by the Initiators. The Initiators are excited about the potential of the change. They have adopted it long before the Defenders. They also do not like hearing the concerns raised by the Defenders. But, if the organization has not been polarized, the Defenders can play their role effectively, contributing to the organization's health. Facilitators can help Defenders and Initiators experience conflict productively rather than divisively by using the Conflict Resolution Process.

Alternatives to the "resistance" label

The "resistance" label automatically calls for "overcoming the opposition." As we have seen, this label is not productive. There are good alternatives. One such alternative is "conflict." Naming the behavior of a Defender as conflict or as a difference of opinion directs a group's attention to the Conflict Resolution Process. Groups that have experienced success with this process know that differences provide new ideas and new thinking. The Defender is no longer slapped with a negative level and dismissed as a problem. He or she is an equal partner in creating a resolution that will better serve the group and the organization.

A group charged with improving how sales contact information is collected appeared to be brought to a halt by two factions of the group. One was advocating a completely new process, whereas the other backed keeping the old system with a few minor modifications. The facilitator became aware of the conflict and said, "We appear to have a conflict on this issue and it will be hard for us to complete our assignment if we get stuck here. Is everyone in agreement that we need to resolve this conflict?" Everyone in the group agreed. "Can we reaffirm our agreement from last meeting about what we require this system to be able to do?" Again, the group agreed. "Let's have every group member state what they believe to be essential to the process we are developing." Both the advocates for a new process and the proponents of the current process were able to share their views. They discovered they were not in such disagreement as they first thought, and the two sides were able to resolve the sticking points.

In most conflict situations people do not feel that their concerns and positions are heard and respected. Using the Conflict Resolution Process gives everyone an opportunity to express himself or herself and be acknowledged. This is all that is needed before the members and the group can move forward to a resolution.

The behaviors and attitudes associated with "resistance" are flags that help identify problems with changes. There is usually a lot of personal ego invested in major change efforts. Individuals have worked hard trying to create the most effective change, and they take critical comments very personally. They may perceive such comments as reflecting badly on their capabilities. Initiators may snap back at negative comments. However, if the goal of this effort is to create the most effective change, then input from a Defender should be considered a sign of Collaboration, even Co-Ownership. The Defenders could remain quiet and let the change fail. What appears to be opposition may, in fact, be support. As mentioned earlier, this supportive intent is less likely in a coercive or competitive environment. If it is real support, the facilitator can help draw out the concerns and help everyone integrate the new information.

Effective facilitators understand change

Effective facilitators help groups use the various change models to get their work done and work together more effectively. They help groups improve their ability to deal with change. They do this by:

- Listening for signals and asking questions
- Identifying forces for change and forces for stability
- Helping group members work through the stages of change
- Helping Initiators, Majority, and Defenders listen to one another and find their common ground
- Coaching their groups to identify the many systems that may be affected by a change
- Avoiding the temptation to label people as "resistors"

Do facilitators have to do all of these things all at once? Of course not. That is not possible. Effective facilitators keep this portfolio of models handy in order to help a group work through its problems and get its work done.

Change is a normal part of the life of groups. Facilitators who are prepared to help groups deal effectively with change provide an immediate and useful service. Groups are better able to respond to changes initiated in the larger organization and to create changes that help them be more productive. Group members feel more comfortable with the changes happening in their lives and can fully participate in the work and life of their groups.

Quick Fix: Solutions to Common Problems

In this chapter you will learn:

- Easily used solutions to common problems
- To translate observations into action
- What behaviors to look for to understand problems
- Some of the underlying issues in common problems
- Where to find more information in this book

*A*ll facilitators confront challenging situations. Overbearing participants, late arrivals at meetings, and serious conflicts among group members can really knock a group off track. If the facilitator does not take appropriate action, the group will spiral downward. Although there is no single "right" way to respond to these problems, effective facilitators give themselves a number of good options. And, they have a knack for choosing the ones that work.

How do facilitators know what to do about these problems? They are alert to the signals from the group. They know what to watch for, and their observations reveal the issues behind the behaviors they see. Once they uncover the underlying issues, effective facilitators help groups deal with them in productive ways.

In this chapter we give you possible solutions to 15 common problems faced by facilitators. We call these solutions "Quick Fixes" because they give you immediate assistance—recommendations for what to do to help the group. Each Quick Fix refers you to a part of the book where you can find more in-depth information.

Look for the following elements in each Quick Fix:

- Example of the problem
- What to watch for
- What issues may be underlying what you observe
- Comments about the nature of the problem
- Actions for the facilitator and group to take to address the problem
- Where to go in the book for more help

Find the problems that are most challenging for you. Look at the action suggested. Which ones have you already been doing? Which ones might you try? Test them out. Follow the trail back into the book to learn more about the dynamics of these situations. The most effective facilitators experiment; they try different approaches. When one works, they may use it again. When one doesn't work, they try something else. The primary question is, "How will the action help the group get back on task?"

It is important to remember that *problems are not isolated incidents.* All group interactions and behaviors take place in a larger context of patterns of group behavior and organizational and personal influences. Facilitators have the best long-term impact on their groups if they consider these larger contexts.

This chapter will save you time and help you choose actions that have worked for other facilitators. It also shows you how to apply the Facilitation Model and how to manage boundaries and change in real situations. We wish you the best of luck as you help groups solve these and other problems and, most importantly, get their work done.

Q uick Fix solutions for facilitators

Finding the answers you need, fast

Group member behavior problem

Discussion dominated by one or two people

▶ **Example**   As often happened during group meetings, Bill and Sue domi-nated the discussion. They had some good ideas, but the facilitator was sure the other group members also had something to contribute. At times, either Bill or Sue would simply state an opinion as a "fact," leaving no room for an alternative. At other times, they would cut off or ridicule the suggestions of others. Some of the group members were acting frustrated; others had already "checked out" and were no longer interested.

What to watch for:

- Only one or two people are doing all the talking.
- Facilitator senses that other group members have ideas not contributed.
- Facilitator observes group members being cut off and/or ideas ridiculed.
- Group's discussions appear perfunctory.
- Group rarely has several options to discuss.
- Excluded members appear bored.
- Group members appear to be acting differently from behavior observed in other settings.

Underlying issues:

- Group member expectations of each other unclear
- Group Charter not clarified
- Work processes not clear
- Lack of respect for one another
- Role as group member not determined
- Violations of the intellectual boundary
- Group does not know how to conduct effective meetings

Comments:

Addressing the problem of one or more people dominating a group can be especially challenging due to the number of interrelated issues that may be affecting the situation. Groups usually have some people who generate ideas and talk more than others. This is normal. The problem arises when this reaches an extreme and group members are excluded from meaningful participation.

Quick Fix ▶

▶*Quick Fix* *Discussion dominated by one or two people*

Facilitator Action:

- Structure discussions so others can participate. For example,
  - Give each person an opportunity in turn, going around the room.
  - Set up dyad or triad discussions, with results presented to the whole group.
  - Have each individual write suggestions before or during meetings, for dissemination before or at meetings.
- Remind the group of their common purpose (Charter) and need for everyone's participation.
- Initiate a clarification of the work processes.
- Have off-line discussions with dominating individuals about observations.

Group Action:

- Create ground rules and/or enforce adherence to them.
- Participate in discussions about Charter and work processes.

Where to go for more help

Issue	Chapter	What to learn there
Group member expectations of each other unclear	5	*Clarifying expectations:* How do expectations of each other affect performance?
Group Charter not clarified	2	*How to create a Charter:* How is a Charter created that describes a group's purpose, goals, roles, and procedures?
Work processes not clear	2	*Defining work processes:* What is the impact of unclear processes? How can they be developed, clarified, or refined?
Lack of respect for one another	4	*Dealing with differences:* How does a group benefit from differences? How should this concept be integrated with work processes?
Role as group member not determined	2	*Group member roles:* How is each group member going to contribute to the success of the whole group? How is the group going to support members successfully fulfilling their role?
Violations of the intellectual boundary	9	*Intellectual boundaries:* What is an intellectual boundary? How does honoring this boundary contribute to success?
Group does not know how to conduct effective meetings	7	*Effective meetings:* What constitutes an effective meeting? Introduce PAL. How do you plan for a productive meeting?

Group member behavior problem

Too many "zingers"

▶ **Example**   When Joe lost an important customer, Sharon laughed and said, "Nice going, Joe. Why don't you see if you can get rid of *all* of your customers! Then we won't have to work as hard." Joe shot back, "I'm really looking forward to the day when I can walk on water like you, Sharon." Throughout the work day, group members regularly made disparaging remarks like this about each other, the topic of discussion, and so on. They claimed they were "just kidding" and "didn't really mean anything by it." When asked about these *zingers*, most members of the group defended this way of communicating. "This is just the way we talk to each other. Nobody takes it seriously."

What to watch for:

- Humor is often at the expense of one or more group members.
- Zingers are often traded back and forth within a group.
- Group members portray zingers as a preferred way they communicate with each other.
- Facilitator notices group members withdrawing after receiving a zinger.

Underlying issues:

- Nature of interpersonal relationships
- Style of communication to be used
- How far on the Group Development Curve the group wishes to progress
- Work processes to be followed
- Commitment of members to group success
- Facilitator needs to use Self to judge whether a comment is a zinger

Comments:

Many groups and group members use zingers as a major form of communication. Those who give zingers often describe them as humorous ways to show affection. Some people are much more effective in creating zingers than others. They use zingers to establish dominance in a group and to protect themselves from the zingers of others. Others will use zingers more rarely and usually in self-defense. Whether or not people are aware of the negative effects of a zinger, it is a direct blow at an individual's sense of self-worth, capability, and value to the group, and is not a helpful communication.

Quick Fix ▶

▶*Quick Fix* *Too many "zingers"*

Facilitator Action:

- Monitor Self for reaction to comments.
- Share with the group your own experience of the zingers.
- If the group does not suggest it, then suggest a ban on zingers as an addition to the ground rules.
- Help the group to understand the counterproductive nature of zingers.
- Invite group members to share how zingers feel to them and support their sharing the painful or angry side of zingers.

Group Action:

- Include a ban on zingers in the group's ground rules.
- Rigorously enforce this ban.
- Explore how the group can communicate and share humor in less destructive ways.
- Review how they expect to work together.

Where to go for more help

Issue	Chapter	What to learn there
Nature of interpersonal relationships	5	*The 6C Relationship Model:* The different types of relationships and how those various relationships impact individual and group performance.
Style of communication to be used	5	*Effective small group communication:* Building on the 6C Relationship Model: the different styles of communicating and their effect on group performance.
How far on the Group Development Curve the group wishes to progress	5	*Group Development Curve model:* The different types of groups, their productivity and interdependence characteristics, and what groups can do to improve both.
Work processes to be followed	3	*Work processes* that will help the group work more effectively together.
Commitment of members to group success	7	*A clear Charter,* creating alignment with a common goal and individual roles in creating group success.
Facilitator needs to use Self to judge whether a comment is a zinger	2	*Using Self as an instrument:* Key ways a facilitator can safely expect his or her own experience to parallel the experience of the group.

Group member behavior problem

Leader or manager breaks rules

▶ **Example**   Jim is the manager, but not the facilitator, of several work groups. He has juggled this responsibility with his many other assignments. Although Jim was present when the group agreed to its ground rules, he frequently has violated them. He has been consistently late to meetings and often has left early. Jim has interrupted others, either interjecting his thoughts or trying to hurry up discussion. He has not been willing to talk about how his behavior has negatively affected the group. His behavior has been very frustrating for both the group and the facilitator.

What to watch for:

- Ground rules are not being honored.
- Violator is not willing to talk about the problem.
- Some group members appear to fear making a contribution.
- Some group members are now skipping meetings due to other pressing responsibilities.
- Key work of the group is not being completed on schedule.
- Group members spend nonmeeting time complaining about the conduct of the manager or leader.

Underlying issues:

- Group purpose is not clear and/or accepted
- Accountability is weak
- Group needs to establish or reaffirm its procedures
- Roles in group are not clear, including that of the manager
- Group's process for resolving conflict needs attention
- Ground rules, work process, and intellectual boundary violations

Comments:

Enforcing ground rules can be a challenging problem, especially when the manager is the primary culprit. Raising the issue can become a quagmire. The difficulty arises because it often is defined as a power struggle. The manager may feel the need to win such a struggle. The biggest challenge here is to redefine the discussion in terms of the issues, especially *why are we here* and *how will we work together* to be successful. This will be more difficult if the facilitator is personally vulnerable to retribution from the manager.

Quick Fix ▶

▶*Quick Fix* *Leader or manager breaks rules*

Facilitator Action:

- Review the group's ground rules and gain commitment to each one.
- Meet in private with the manager and reaffirm or clarify:
  - Charge to the group
  - Commitment to success of the group
  - Process the group has agreed to follow
  - Manager's understanding of her or his unique role in the group
  - Manager's expectations of the group
- Reaffirm group's Charter or agree to create one.
- Reaffirm group's process for addressing conflict or agree to create one.

Group Action:

- Fully participate in reaffirmation or establishment of group's Charter.
- Fully participate in reaffirmation or establishment of group's process for working through conflict.
- Discuss ground rules and agree to rules that they can feel commitment to uphold.

Where to go for more help

Issue	Chapter	What to learn there
Group purpose is not clear and/or accepted	1	*Clarifying why the group is together:* For what is it being held accountable? This is the purpose in the group's Charter.
Accountability is weak	2	*Building accountability:* Review the group's Charter.
Group needs to establish or reaffirm its procedures	2	*Establishing work procedures:* What are their impact on the group? How can they be developed, clarified, or refined?
Roles in group are not clear, including that of the manager	2	*Defining roles:* Using group goals to clarify expectations and define roles. How can individuals be held accountable?
Group's process for resolving conflict needs attention	6	*Resolving conflict:* How is each group member going to contribute to the success of the whole group? How can group members be supported in successfully fulfilling their role?
Ground rules, work process, and intellectual boundary violations	9	*Ground rules, work process, and intellectual boundaries:* How does honoring them contribute to a group's success?

Group member behavior problem

Breaches of confidence

Example   George had just gone through a very painful divorce and, not surprisingly, it was affecting his work performance. He revealed a number of personal facts to two trusted and close group members. He asked that the information be held in confidence. They agreed to say nothing to others. Within a few days, however, it became evident that much of this information had been shared. It was becoming general knowledge in the organization. Someone had breached the confidence.

What to watch for:

- Confidential private information has become public knowledge.
- Group members become less willing to share information.
- Group interactions become more strained.
- Group members choose to work alone rather than collaboratively.
- Resolving conflicts becomes more difficult.
- A group member states that a confidence has been broken.

Underlying issues:

- Trust among group members has been damaged
- Group's ability to work collaboratively has been weakened
- Confidence is reduced that agreements will be upheld
- Commitment to one another is questioned
- Privacy, ground rules, and group process ground rules have been violated

Comments:

Especially when sensitive information has been shared, such a breach in confidence can have a very negative effect on the group. Effective groups require a high level of trust among members. When a breach occurs, members are less likely to work collaboratively (e.g., share information that affects their performance and/or their relationships with other group members.) They also tend to distrust members about completing agreed upon tasks. Although it may not be important to name the "guilty" party, such breaches of confidence must be addressed quickly and directly.

Quick Fix ▶

▎*Quick Fix* Breaches of confidence

Facilitator Action:

- Name the fact that a breach of confidence has occurred.
- Structure a discussion to help the group acknowledge both the breach and the effect it has already had on the group. Be prepared to deal with "fall-out."
- Structure a discussion for the group to review its agreements about maintaining confidences.
- Help the group reaffirm its commitment to fulfilling its Charter.
- Support the group in reaffirming its commitment to working collaboratively.

Group Action:

- If not already included, add a confidentiality element in the ground rules.
- Review the group's Charter, including those sections about how members will work together.
- Reaffirm their commitment to work together in a collaborative manner, including respecting each other's privacy.
- Share personal reactions or the impact of information being shared.

Where to go for more help

Issue	Chapter	What to learn there
Trust among group members has been damaged	5	*Building trust:* What actions can be taken to build and/or rebuild trust?
Group's ability to work collaboratively has been weakened	5	*6C Relationship Model:* What are the various relationship styles that appear in groups? What is the impact of collaboration on the productivity of a group?
Confidence is reduced that agreements will be upheld	6	*Conflict Resolution Process:* Fulfilling agreements is part of a group's process. Dealing with resistance and managing conflict are addressed.
Commitment to one another is questioned	2	*Group Charter:* Nature of the Charter and the steps to follow to create, modify, or reaffirm it.
Privacy, ground rules, and group process ground rules have been violated	9	*Privacy, ground rules, and group process boundaries:* How does honoring them contribute to a group's success?

Group is "stuck"

Group has difficulty completing work

Example   Sue looked around the group in frustration. She had been sure the group would finally be able to check off a task as "completed." But, just as they were within reach of the end, Bill diverted the group. He had a "crisis" and needed the group's attention immediately. Everyone responded, and the first project was left undone. If history repeated itself, it would be very hard to get the group back on the first task to complete it. They would probably get diverted from Bill's task, too, before it was done. The group seemed to spin its wheels without results.

What to watch for:

- Units of work are not completed before attention moves to another unit of work.
- Backlog of work to be completed continues to grow.
- Supervisors are expressing concern over lack of work completed.
- Group members often point fingers at others as the cause of lack of output.
- Group members complain about being overloaded.
- The group is interfered with by nongroup members.
- Organization's priorities change.

Underlying issues:

- Group is unclear about managing accountability
- Group needs a useful Charter
- Group has not clarified how it will know that a unit of work is completed
- Group cannot prioritize tasks
- Group needs a process for creating clear sets of steps to complete each unit of work
- Group has not identified a way to celebrate work completed
- Group needs to decide how to deal with others
- Group's Charge has changed

Comments:

Groups in work settings are created to complete tasks. Failing to complete work has consequences for individuals, groups, leaders, and the whole organization. Frequently groups focus on the easier, low-priority tasks while more important work remains uncompleted. Groups that do not get their work done need to pay attention to their Charge and Charter. They have to be clear on their purpose, goals, roles, and procedures. Each group member, as well as the whole group, is accountable for productivity. Outside interference or changes in organizational priorities will require group action.

Quick Fix ▶

▶*Quick Fix* Group has difficulty completing work

Facilitator Action:

- Name the fact that key work is not being completed.
- Structure a discussion to help the group acknowledge both this failure and the effect it has already had on the group.
- Structure a discussion for the group to review its Charge and Charter.
- Help the group either reaffirm or modify its existing Charter.
- Support the group in developing and using a process for monitoring the amount of work completed.
- Introduce the concept of the parking lot so new issues, or tasks that are set aside, can be dealt with *after* the current work is done.
- Support the group in examining how it might be accountable for more than one Charge and what action to take to deal with the situation.

Group Action:

- Acknowledge the failure to complete assigned work and to commit to being more successful in the future.
- Review and affirm or revise the group's Charter, or develop a new one.
- Celebrate the completion of work.
- Monitor work completed.

Where to go for more help

Issue	Chapter	What to learn there
Group is unclear about managing accountability	2	*Clarifying accountability:* Different expectations of group performance by group members and others will cause problems.
Group needs a useful Charter	2	A *group Charter* presents the group's purpose, goals, roles, and procedures.
Group has not clarified how it will know that a unit of work is completed	2	*Identifying work completion:* What units of work will be accomplished? How will accomplishment be measured?
Group cannot prioritize tasks	7	*Prioritizing tasks:* Several useful tools for this process are suggested.
Group needs a process for creating clear steps to complete each work unit	7	*Process mapping:* Several tools for creating clear steps to complete tasks are suggested.
Group has not identified a way to celebrate work completed	5	*Celebrating successes:* Groups can follow some simple processes for creating celebrations. Suggestions of celebrations.
Group needs to decide how to deal with others	9	*Us vs. them boundary:* Group must determine how it expects to relate to others.
Group's Charge has changed	2	*Group Charter:* Group's Charter must be changed to reflect the new Charge.

Group is "stuck"

Group has conflict over priorities

Example   Since they successfully finished the last big project, each group meeting looks and feels like a rerun of previous meetings. The meetings seem to proceed without clear direction as various group members argue over what the group should tackle next. Some members remain silent, but most take sides. People are complaining that nothing is getting done but they won't budge on what task to do next. The department director has given the group no guidance beyond the admonition to be productive.

What to watch for:

- There is no agreement on the next task to be completed.
- Individuals and groups take sides on the issue but fail to reach an agreement.
- Meetings seem to proceed without any clear purpose.
- Group members complain about the lack of progress.
- Group members appear to be growing less committed to the success of the group.
- Group receives conflicting direction about priorities.

Underlying issues:

- Group may lack process for establishing priorities
- Charge is unclear or later communications add ambiguity
- No clear Charter developed by group for this time
- Group may have needed a breather after the last project
- Meetings are not effective
- Group needs to have a process for dealing with conflict more effectively

Comments:

An inability to set priorities occurs most often when the Charge to the group is insufficient or nonexistent. It also may happen when a group has been in existence for a longer period of time and has had a pattern of creating its own assignments. Groups that have had to rise to a very big challenge often find they crash after they have been successful. At the core of this problem is the lack of a clear sense of why they are still together. It is from this collective sense of purpose that priorities become clearer.

Quick Fix ▶

▶ *Quick Fix* Group has conflict over priorities

Facilitator Action:

- Name the conflict and its disabling effect on the group.
- Support the group requesting clarification of their Charge.
- Structure a process for the group to create or modify its Charter.
- Structure an opportunity for the group to explore its approach to conflict and develop a more effective conflict management process.
- Introduce one or more of the prioritization tools to resolve the current conflict.
- Use Conflict Resolution Process.

Group Action:

- Commit to and then act on creating or modifying its Charter.
- Commit to and act on creating or modifying conflict management process.
- Adopt the PAL (Purpose–Agenda–Logistics) system for meetings.
- Use Conflict Resolution Process.

Where to go for more help

Issue	Chapter	What to learn there
Group may lack process for establishing priorities	7	*Priority setting process:* Setting priorities can be a much easier task when using one of the tools, such as multi-voting.
Charge is unclear or later communications add ambiguity	2	*Clarify Charge:* The impact of a clear Charge on a group. How does the Charge contribute to a productive Charter development process?
No clear Charter developed by group for this time	2	*Develop Charter:* The Charter development process addresses the issues of purpose, goals, roles, and procedures.
Group may have needed a breather after the last project	5	*Group Development Curve:* Describes the dangers of a major success and how a group can succeed again.
Meetings are not effective	7	*PAL:* The PAL meeting process can contribute to more effective meetings
Group needs to have a process for dealing with conflict more effectively	6	*Conflict Resolution Process:* Helps individuals and groups understand their styles in dealing with conflict. Conflict management process helps groups use conflict to their advantage.

Group is "stuck"

Group has conflict over the use of resources

▶**Example**   Bob and Natasha were responsible for coordinating the work
on two different sections of their group's project. They were expected to utilize the time and talent of other group members, as needed. Bill, the facilitator, could hear the two arguing again. He had lost track of the times during
the past few weeks that they had fought over who was going to get the
time of one of the group members. Bill had tried to talk with each of them,
but that hadn't stopped the conflict. Their arguing was now putting the project behind schedule.

What to watch for:

• The conflict repeats itself without any resolution.
• Other group members appear to be avoiding contact with the combatants.
• Progress on assigned tasks is falling behind schedule.
• Cooperation among other group members is declining.

Underlying issues:

• Process needed for resolving conflicts
• Overall task not the top priority
• Roles and their complementary nature not clear
• Violation of use of resources boundary

Comments:

There is always a limit on the resources available to a group. In a work environment where a dominant paradigm is stiff competition for scarce
resources, it is often difficult for group members to readily share resources
needed to complete tasks within the group. The difficulty is greatly
increased when the group will not take the time to create effective work
procedures that include how resources will be shared. The very competitive
drive and habits that contribute to the conflicts often block productive discussions about work processes. The Conflict Resolution Process can help
groups resolve disputes about the use of scarce resources.

Quick Fix ▶

▌*Quick Fix* Group has conflict over the use of resources

Facilitator Action:

- Name the conflict and help the group use the Conflict Resolution Process.
- Assist the group in reaffirming its Charter, or if none, lead the group in creating one.
- Assist the group in reaffirming its procedures for sharing resources, or if none, lead the group in creating one. This includes giving a priority for the use of each resource.
- Focus the group on why they are together and how individual success is tied to overall success.

Group Action:

- Use the Conflict Resolution Process.
- Reaffirm or create a group Charter.
- Reaffirm or create work procedures for sharing resources.

Where to go for more help

Issue	Chapter	What to learn there
Process needed for resolving conflicts	6	*Conflict Resolution Process:* Individual Conflict Mode preferences and how members can make appropriate choices for particular situations.
Overall task not the top priority	2	*Group Charge:* Clarification of the Charge helps group members understand their accountability.
Roles and their complementary nature not clear	2	*Group member roles:* An important part of a group's Charter is the assignment of roles to group members. Roles clarify who is to do what and how they relate to others.
Violation of use of resources boundary	9	*Use of resources boundary:* Limits on how resources are to be used become a boundary. Violation of that boundary leads to conflict and reduced effectiveness in reaching goals.

Group is "stuck"

"Resisting" change

▶**Example**   Dale's group had really been thrown by the restructuring announcement it had received three weeks earlier. The group had been working well on achieving its goals when it was suddenly given a new task and new people. Every meeting since the announcement has focused mainly on complaints about the new direction. Dale and a couple of group members could see the benefits of the change, but the rest would not accept it. The group's ability to get work done had simply disappeared.

What to watch for:

- Group members spend significant time complaining about a change.
- Work associated with the change is not getting done as required.
- Group members begin to miss meetings or arrive late.
- Group members may appear listless and/or disengaged.
- Group members may actively attempt to restore the old.
- Group members may simply continue completing their old tasks.

Underlying issues:

- Group members' sense of their own identity has been challenged
- Group members are being asked to leave the known for the unknown
- Group members may be grieving over their loss
- Group members may deny that change has taken place
- Group members may identify aspects of the old that should be retained
- Revised Charge requires revisions in the Charter

Comments:

Significant changes can be a shock to groups and group members, especially when they have had little or no input into the nature of the change. Normal responses to such changes are often interpreted as "resistance" and the people called "resisters" when they are actually behaving normally. It is normal for people to experience denial and grief about a major change. Not accepting the change may be healthy for the organization. Because individuals complete change processes at different paces, this also may look like "resistance." A facilitator can help people understand the change process and successfully respond to it. Most "resistance" will fade when this has happened. The group can then get on with its work.

Quick Fix ▶

Quick Fix *"Resisting" change*

Facilitator Action:

- Name the change as a loss that must be grieved.
- Acknowledge the need to take time to complete the grieving process.
- Create opportunities for group members to acknowledge and feel their grief; simple rituals are helpful in this process.
- Structure a discussion to identify what aspects of the change may legitimately be challenged—too much may have been "thrown out."
- Structure an opportunity for the group to review its Charter in light of the new Charge and make appropriate revisions.
- Monitor the behavior of group members for further evidence that they are not able to move forward.

Group Action:

- Acknowledge the loss and participate in the grieving process.
- Support each other in completing the grief process and move on.
- Identify what aspects of the change may legitimately be challenged and create an appropriate plan of action.
- Review and revise the group Charter in light of the Charge.

Where to go for more help

Issue	Chapter	What to learn there
Group members' sense of their own identity has been challenged	10	*Impact of change on identity:* How individuals' identities are intertwined with their work. Take steps to help them revise or renew their sense of identity.
Group members are being asked to leave the known for the unknown	10	*Loss of competency:* They were experts in what they had been doing and are now novices at what they must do.
Group members may be grieving over their loss	10	*Grief process:* There are many things a facilitator can do to help individuals progress through the grief process.
Group members may deny that change has taken place	10	*Impact of denial:* Some individuals may act as if the change never happened.
Group members may identify aspects of the old that should be retained	10	*Defender role:* Blindly accepting all aspects of change may not be in the best interest of the organization.
Revised Charge requires revisions in the Charter	2	*Charge and Charter:* The Charge to the group has changed. The purpose, goals, roles, and procedures may now change.

Group is "stuck":

Group member(s) too angry to work

Example   For the second consecutive meeting, Dave's loud outbursts about the reorganization were keeping the group from working on the capital equipment order. "I can't believe they took away our group's project engineer. The so-called engineering consultant they gave us is clueless. How in hell are we supposed to complete this capital equipment P.O.?" A few other people got caught up in Dave's anger, too. They were focused more on complaining and less on completing the P.O. The equipment delivery lead time was already bumping up against the project timetable, and the vendor needed the signed P.O. to ship. Because they were stuck in their anger, the group had ground to a halt.

What to watch for:

- One or more group member's expressions of anger disrupt the group.
- One or more group members' attention is fixed on something that upsets them.
- Personal or organizational changes continue to be upsetting to one or more group members.
- The work of the group is not completed due to these disruptions.
- Individuals question their own future role with the organization.

Underlying issues:

- Emotions in the workplace are a normal part of group life
- Changes can have a very disruptive effect on individuals and groups
- Individuals and groups need processes for addressing strong feelings
- Major organizational changes may have invalidated the group's Charge and Charter
- Individuals, disturbed by changes, need to reassess their personal capabilities and roles
- Emotional boundary may be violated

Comments:

Emotions are always present in the workplace and always affect work performance, negatively or positively. Expressions of anger are often difficult for groups because most organizations' cultural norms do not support such expressions. Everyone is expected to "keep under control." Dealing with feelings is not recognized as a business activity. Therefore, processes are not readily available to help an individual or group work through such feelings. Anger is often disturbing to facilitators and group members because it creates a sense of helplessness, and they are not able to make it "go away."

Quick Fix ▶

▶ *Quick Fix* *Group member(s) too angry to work*

Facilitator Action:

- Progress on other tasks will not occur until the anger is directly dealt with in the group. Name the experience of anger.
- Focus the attention of the group on addressing how to support their fellow group members in dealing with their feelings of anger.
- Help the group develop a process for moving through the emotional issues and then returning to the work to be done.
- Help the group to understand the stages of change and what activities are necessary to move through them.
- Help the group to reassess the continuing validity of its Charge and Charter and modify where necessary.
- In a severe case, a private, sensitive suggestion of outside counseling may be made.

Group Action:

- Acknowledge the strong emotions and the need to address them directly before other work can be completed.
- Use a process for supporting upset group members and then work through the emotional issues.
- Reassess the Charge and Charter and modify where necessary.

Where to go for more help

Issue	Chapter	What to learn there
Emotions in the work-place are a normal part of group life	3	*Impact of emotions* on groups. Benefits to be gained by acknowledging the emotions.
Changes can have a very disruptive effect on individuals and groups	10	*Stages of change:* Individuals, as well as groups, experience stages of change where needs and capabilities differ.
Individuals and groups need processes for ad-dressing strong feelings	5	*Expressing emotions:* Productive ways for groups to address strong feelings and achieve positive outcomes.
Major organizational changes may have inval-idated the group's Charge and Charter	2	*Charge and Charter:* For what is the group now accountable? What will be its purpose, goals, roles, and procedures to fulfill its new Charge?
Individuals, disturbed by changes, need to reassess their personal capabilities and roles	10	*Adjusting to change:* How might change erode an individual's self-esteem and what can be done about it.
Emotional boundary may be violated	9	*Emotion boundary:* Limits on expression of emotions is a boundary. Violation can have a variety of effects on groups.

Group has process problems

Group member(s) too busy to discuss process

Example   Rob, the facilitator, had lost count of the times the group reinvented a process for a similar problem. Each time he had called attention to this pattern and suggested the group take the time to develop a good process. The response had always been the same. Several group members, especially Tom and Judy, would say, "We don't have time for that soft, 'touchy-feely' stuff. We have work to be done." The total time lost due to lack of having a good process had far exceeded the time the group would have needed to develop one.

What to watch for:

- Work is not completed efficiently or on time due to lack of a good process.
- Process discussions are characterized as a waste of time by group members.
- Group members assume that everyone knows how to complete some particular work.
- Group members assume that everyone is in agreement about how to do some particular work.
- Group members continue to act as independent individuals rather than as members of the group.
- Meetings are described as a waste of time.

Underlying issues:

- Group members do not understand the role of process in achieving success
- Group members have little experience consciously creating process
- Group members do not perceive how procedures can help them be productive
- Consciously creating a process is a change in behavior
- No effective process for running meetings

Comments:

Being attentive to process is often far outside the operating paradigm of groups. They not only fail to see the value of process, they exert a lot of effort to thwart even talking about it. As individuals, they have created processes and used them, but usually on a subconscious level. They prefer to do-it-as-they-go. For a group to have a process requires everyone to consciously think of the steps required and talk about them. This can be a radical departure from past behaviors.

Quick Fix ▶

Quick Fix *Group member(s) too busy to discuss process*

Facilitator Action:

- Name the problem as lack of process and explain the price the group is paying for not developing one.
- Name the difficulty in changing from their more individually oriented behaviors.
- Assist the group in understanding that developing a specific process for the current situation has raised this issue again. Use this process as a way for the group to test the validity of consciously creating processes.
- Suggest an effective meetings process as a good place to start.

Group Action:

- Acknowledge the lack of success arising from the failure to have a process.
- Affirm their collective accountability for the group's success.
- Test the process development procedure for its validity.

Where to go for more help

Issue	Chapter	What to learn there
Group members do not understand the role of process in achieving success	7	*Fundamental work processes* play a crucial role in successfully completing work.
Group members have little experience consciously creating process	5	*Group participation* differs from acting as an independent individual.
Group members do not perceive how procedures can help them be productive	2	*Creating group procedures* differs from creating individual procedures.
Consciously creating a process is a change in behavior	10	*Change processes:* How individuals as well as groups make or resist changes. How this process of change is a sequential series of decisions rather than a one-time yes or no.
No effective process for running meetings	7	*Running effective meeting:* PAL is an easy-to-use process that gets results.

Group has process problems

Members not contributing

Example   Denise looked around the table at the faces staring blankly back at her. She was tired. As the facilitator, Denise had been working very hard to help this group. She had been trying for an hour to engage its members in a discussion about how they were going to complete their major task. A couple of people had responded with very brief comments to questions or requests directed specifically to them. Otherwise, no one was contributing. Denise knew she had to find a way to get everyone engaged or their work would not get done.

What to watch for:

- Group members appear reluctant to contribute ideas.
- The facilitator has to work very hard to gain much participation.
- Group members appear to be distracted and not talking.
- Group members talk actively in other settings.
- Group members appear to be paying attention but not talking.
- Group members are usually quiet in other settings too.

Underlying issues:

- Group members may not be committed to the work of the group
- Appropriate process for gaining participation may not have been developed by group
- Facilitator may be unconsciously discouraging participation by others
- Some group member(s) may be influencing others not to contribute
- Group members may be more introverted, requiring different forms of participation

Comments:

Lack of contribution by group members can be caused by a number of underlying issues. A trap for facilitators is to feel totally responsible for group productivity, including participation by individuals. Facilitators are responsible for creating a setting where participation is easier for members. An ineffective meeting process makes it harder for members to participate. However, group members are responsible for their own participation and output. It is helpful for a facilitator to consider several diagnostic questions. Is the lack of participation a change from the previous pattern? How do group members act in other settings? Would group members be more likely to contribute if they could do it in dyads or triads? Would producing their contributions in writing be better? Once some of these questions are answered, the facilitator can have the group decide how they want to achieve more participation.

Quick Fix

▶*Quick Fix* *Members not contributing*

Facilitator Action:

- Assess the nature of the lack of contributions.
- Structure the opportunities for participation, if appropriate.
- Initiate a group discussion about the ways they want to participate.
- Initiate a review of the Charge and Charter.
- Monitor the pattern of contribution.
- Have the group assess its participation.
- Have the group assess its meeting process.

Group Action:

- Acknowledge how the lack of participation has impacted group performance.
- Review the Charge and Charter and, if necessary, modify the Charter.
- Review the work processes and, if necessary, modify them.
- Commit to contributing to the degree necessary for the group to be successful.

Where to go for more help

Issue	Chapter	What to learn there
Group members may not be committed to the work of the group	2	*Charge and Charter:* Examining why a group is together and the steps necessary to be successful.
Appropriate process for gaining participation may not have been developed by group	7	*Work processes:* Developing and reviewing the processes required to complete the work.
Facilitator may be unconsciously blocking participation by others	3	*Impact of facilitator:* How facilitators can use themselves consciously to avoid damaging actions and promote productivity.
Some group member(s) may be influencing others not to contribute	5	*6C Relationship Model:* How different relationships affect the productivity of a group.
Group members may be more introverted, requiring different forms of participation	4	*Social styles:* How personal style preferences impact the way work can be completed in groups.

Group has process problems

Group always goes directly to solutions

Example   The problem was barely presented before several group members began to suggest ways to solve it. This was a very action-oriented group. It had a full agenda and nearly everyone expressed the need to keep moving. As facilitator, Ted appreciated the group's ability to get work done, but he was concerned. This was a complex problem. Nevertheless the group was acting as if it had all the information needed to identify the best solution. One member stated she felt the problem needed more in-depth study but her assessment was dismissed by other members. Ted expressed his concern they were not following a good problem-solving process but several group members rejected that idea because they didn't have time for such a process. He reminded them that in the past they had had to reconsider a number of problems because their solutions were inadequate.

What to watch for:

- Group members rush to suggest solutions.
- Individual group members appear to be competing to be first in suggesting a workable solution.
- Group members do not ask questions to learn more about the problem.
- Group appears to be in a rush to move to the next task.
- Group does not come to agreement about how to collect more information.
- Group does not come to agreement about how to solve this problem.
- Group does not agree on criteria for evaluating solutions.
- Group members' concerns are dismissed without real consideration.

Underlying issues:

- Group has difficulty discerning complex from simple problems
- Group members have difficulty hearing important information from others
- Group does not have a process for determining how to solve problems
- Group may not connect problems with achievement of group Charter
- Group has not learned to appreciate differences in the group
- Group has not developed as a Fully Functioning Group

Comments:

At times, everyone has too little time to complete work. Pressure on individuals and groups is intense: Finish this task and get on to the next. People who would like to be more thorough struggle with the pressure to keep moving. Thus, a systematic problem-solving process often is considered a waste of time. When groups think about solving problems, they usually agree that some require a more systematic process. They need to gather information so they can make informed decisions. Unless there was prior agreement about how to solve problems, the pressure will cause groups to be too hasty.

Quick Fix ▶

Quick Fix *Group always goes directly to solutions*

Facilitator Action:

- Assess whether the situation is unique or a common pattern.
- Assess whether the Charter process was completed satisfactorily.
- If it was satisfactory, remind the group of agreements about evaluating problems and developing solutions.
- If it was unsatisfactory, use this situation as an opportunity for the group to learn the importance of developing and using good problem-solving techniques.
- Call attention to the ways group members discourage the participation of others.
- Encourage the group to work in a more collaborative way.

Group Action:

- Acknowledge the focus on solutions.
- Review the Charge and Charter and, if necessary, modify the Charter.
- Review the ways members relate to each other and decide how they can work together more effectively.
- Commit to taking the time necessary to develop improved solutions.

Where to go for more help

Issue	Chapter	What to learn there
Group has difficulty discerning complex from simple problems	2	*Charter:* The development of a Charter provides a structure for identifying the problems to be solved.
Group members have difficulty hearing important information from others	8	*Listening:* Assessing how well a person listens and what can be done to improve it.
Group does not have a process for determining how to solve problems	7	*Work processes:* Solving problems is one of the fundamental work processes for groups.
Group may not connect particular problems with achievement of group Charter	2	*Charge and Charter:* A key part of the Charge and Charter process is linking problems and activities to fulfillment of the group's Charge.
Group has not learned to appreciate differences in the group	4	*Social styles:* How different people's styles contribute to the effectiveness of groups.
Group has not developed as a Fully Functioning Group	5	*Group Development Curve:* What action groups need to take in order to develop into a Fully Functioning Group.

Group has process problems

Members have conflicts over expectations of each other

Example   Sandra was furious with Bob. She clearly remembered Bob was to have investigated the discrepancies in the sales reports. When pressed, she couldn't remember a group discussion about it, but she assumed he would do it because he was the sales representative in the cross-functional group. Bob remembered a concern about the reports but hadn't heard that it was considered serious enough to take the time to track it down. Both felt they were "right" and the other person "wrong." After exchanging derogatory comments, they just glared at each other.

What to watch for:

- Group members have very different memories of the who, what, or when of assignments when they do not state goals clearly.
- Group members make assumptions about each other's roles without having talked about them.
- Group members make assumptions about the concerns of others without having talked about them.
- Group members feel they are "right" and other members "wrong."
- Conflicts between or among group members become a "cold war."

Underlying issues:

- Group has not clarified its goals, roles, and procedures
- Process for assigning tasks is either not clear or not consistently followed
- Procedures for discussing problems and determining appropriate action are either not clear or not consistently followed
- Concerns are not considered a priority to fulfillment of group's purpose as stated in Charter
- Group members are willing to settle for less than a Cooperative, Collaborative, or Co-Ownership relationship
- Group has not established or consistently followed its Conflict Resolution Process

Comments:

Being clear about expectations of each other is one of the greatest challenges for groups. Everyone has the tendency to assume they already know what is expected of them and what is reasonable to expect of others. To take the time to clarify what they assume they already know appears to be a waste of time, especially when there is so much work to be done. The reality is that much more time is lost when people have not made correct assumptions. Because both personal and organizational circumstances change, group members must check out their assumptions and clarify their expectations on a regular basis. Facilitators can help by helping their groups schedule this periodic review.

Quick Fix ▶

Quick Fix *Members have conflicts over expectations of each other*

Facilitator Action:

- If the group has a Charter, remind it of the procedures it has created for setting goals and making assignments.
- If the group does not have a Charter, use this incident as an opportunity to complete the Charge and Charter process.
- Assess the nature of the group's relationship, using TARGET as a guide; initiate activities to help group members work better together.
- Initiate the Conflict Resolution Process to help the parties reconcile.

Group Action:

- Review the group's procedures for setting goals and making assignments.
- Develop a Charter if they have not already done so.
- Assess the nature of the group's relationship, using TARGET as a guide, and decide if the group wishes to change it.
- Initiate the Conflict Resolution Steps to help parties in conflict reconcile.

Where to go for more help

Issue	*Chapter*	*What to learn there*
Group hasn't clarified its goals, roles, and procedures	2	*Charge and Charter:* Reaffirm why the group is together and the roles each group member is expected to play to achieve group success.
Process for assigning tasks is either not clear or not consistently followed	2	*Charter:* Review or revise the procedures developed for assignment of tasks.
Procedures for discussing problems and determining appropriate action are either not clear or not consistently followed	2	*Charter:* Review or revise problem-solving procedures identified in the Charter.
	7	*Problem solving:* This fundamental work process utilizes procedures and tools.
Concerns are not considered a priority to fulfillment of group's purpose as stated in Charter	2	*Charge and Charter:* Reaffirm the purpose of the group and the procedures for prioritizing problems and tasks.
Group members are willing to settle for less than a Cooperative, Collaborative, or Co-Ownership relationship	5	*6C Relationship Model:* How different relationships affect the productivity of a group.
Group has not established or consistently followed its Conflict Resolution Process	6	*Conflict Resolution Process:* How conflict can be addressed quickly and successfully.

Special challenges for facilitators

Members arrive late / leave early

▶**Example**   Tom, the group's facilitator, looked with disbelief at the figure slipping out of the door. There was so much work for the group to complete, yet they were too often having to delay action because one of the group members hadn't yet arrived or had already left. A few people did it the most, but recently others were taking the same liberty. Members who were always there were frustrated. Because the problem was getting worse, Tom was increasingly sure the group would not finish its work by its deadline.

What to watch for:

- Group members do not follow the group ground rule for arriving on time.
- Group members do not appear concerned with the completion of the group's work.
- Group members are getting frustrated with the apparent lack of commitment of others.
- Group members grumble about the late arrivals and early departures, but take no further action.
- Conflict among group members is increasing without resolution.

Underlying issues:

- Arriving late/leaving early behavior disruptive to group
- Group members may not be committed to work of the group
- Other demands on members' time may have changed
- Process for holding group members accountable not established or consistently followed
- Members not working cooperatively or collaboratively
- Conflict Resolution Process not used
- Members may give other systems a higher ranking than the group system

Comments:

Competing demands on group members' time is nearly always a problem . It is a real challenge for groups to have candid discussions about the demands on members' time and what they can commit to realistically. Demands often increase incrementally rather than suddenly. Even if groups have a good discussion about this when they establish their Charter, they do not always talk about it later. Group members who value the work of the group may feel guilt and shame for "letting everyone down" by their behavior. If they cannot renegotiate their participation in the group, they often simply become even less active. Renegotiation may create an opportunity for the group to continue to benefit from their participation although that participation may need to look different from what it was in the past.

Quick Fix ▶

▶**Quick Fix** *Members arrive late / leave early*

Facilitator Action:

- Create opportunities for the group to discuss the problem completely instead of allowing the grumbling to continue.
- Review group's Charter to identify commitments that were made there.
- Review the group's ground rules; suggest the group review them too.
- Create opportunities for members to renegotiate commitments to group.
- Create opportunities for the group to support absent group members in dealing with their competing demands.
- Initiate Conflict Resolution Steps where appropriate.

Group Action:

- Discuss the problem more completely instead of continuing the grumbling.
- Review the group's Charter to identify commitments made there.
- Review and possibly modify the group's ground rules.
- Discuss the commitments made to the group and any changes that have an impact on people fulfilling those commitments.
- Support members who have to be absent as they try to modify competing demands.
- Be willing to initiate Conflict Resolution Steps rather than complaining about other group members.

Where to go for more help

Issue	Chapter	What to learn there
Arriving late/leaving early behavior disruptive to group	7	*Running effective meetings:* How to run effective meetings and enforce meeting ground rules.
Group members may not be committed to work of the group	2	*Charge and Charter:* Examining why a group is together and how members agreed to work together for success.
Other demands on members' time may have changed	2	*Charter:* Group roles may have to be re-negotiated to reflect new circumstances.
Process for holding members accountable not established or consistently followed	3	*Impact of facilitator:* How facilitators can use themselves to avoid damaging actions and promote productivity.
Members not working cooper-atively or collaboratively	5	*6C Relationship Model:* How different relationships affect group's productivity.
Conflict Resolution Process not used	6	*Conflict Resolution Process:* Five steps to successfully resolving conflicts.
Members may give other systems a higher ranking than the group system	5	*Rank order of systems:* How the ways people rank-order the systems of which they are a part influences their choices and behaviors.

Special challenges for facilitators

Influencing a meeting when not the "facilitator"

Example   Judy watched as the meeting took a bad turn. She looked at the group's facilitator and saw uncertainty. Although Judy was not the formal facilitator, she had facilitated enough to realize that this group needed some help right away and the facilitator was unsure what to do. Judy wanted this group to be successful but felt uncomfortable about possibly stepping on the facilitator's toes. She quickly gathered her thoughts and prepared to act.

What to watch for:

- Group members share in the commitment to act in a facilitative manner.
- The facilitator is missing important cues.
- Meetings are much less productive than is possible.
- The facilitator is unsure how to help the group get back on track.
- The facilitator is becoming isolated from the group.
- Group members are beginning to undermine the facilitator.

Underlying issues:

- Group has not committed to fulfilling its Charge
- Group has not developed an effective Charter
- Facilitator has not developed a clear contract with the group
- Group is operating in a Coercive, Confrontational, or Coexistence mode
- Facilitator needs to better understand role of Self as instrument
- Facilitator needs to better understand how to influence group
- Group may respond better, at the moment, to group members acting in a facilitative manner

Comments:

Watching another facilitator struggle with a group is usually awkward for someone who has good facilitation skills. It is especially hard when the observer has an investment in the success of the group. When a decision is made to help, the challenge is to help in ways that aid the group in moving forward without pointing out the failings of the facilitator. Helping does not mean taking control of a meeting. Helping can be as subtle as asking the right question at the right moment or as obvious as naming group behavior as hurting the success of the group. The reality is no facilitator can *always* be aware of every group dynamic or choose the best intervention to make. Every facilitator can benefit from assistance from group members. In a Collaborative or Co-Ownership environment, that assistance can be expected. The further groups advance on the Group Development Curve, the more group members will share in the facilitation. Group members are all committed to acting in a facilitative manner.

Quick Fix ▶

▶*Quick Fix* Influencing a meeting when not the "facilitator"

Facilitative Action by a Group Member:

- Assess the need for a group member to act in a facilitative way.
- Identify action that will help the group both in the short- and long-term.
- Be ready to ask clarifying questions as the first level of intervention.
- Ask such clarifying questions in ways that do not undermine the facilitator's standing in the group.
- Express concerns about group conduct in terms of how they affect you rather than the facilitator.
- Be willing to challenge unproductive behavior.
- Ask for the group to review its Charge and Charter.

Group Action:

- Support facilitative behavior by any and all group members.
- Consider facilitative behavior by group members when negotiating a contract with the facilitator.
- Review the Charge and Charter when helpful.

Where to go for more help

Issue	Chapter	What to learn there
Group hasn't committed to fulfilling its Charge	2	*Charge:* Examining why a group is together and the steps necessary to be successful.
Group has not developed an effective Charter	2	*Charter:* Develop purpose, goals, roles, and procedures that will lead to group success.
Facilitator has not developed a clear contract with the group	1	*Contracting:* Facilitators must identify what a group is expecting of them and create an agreement about how the facilitation will be delivered.
Group is operating in a Coercive, Confrontational, or Coexistence mode	5	*6C Relationship Model:* The win–lose model does not lead to maximum productivity. There are ways to help a group operate in a more partnering way.
Facilitator needs to better understand role of Self as instrument	3	*Self as instrument:* How a facilitator's impact on a group may be different from what is intended.
Facilitator needs to better understand how to influence group	3	*Methods of influencing:* How people influence each other, especially how a facilitator's behavior may contribute to either positive or negative outcomes.
Group may respond better to members acting in a facilitative manner	Intro	*Facilitating from the side:* Appropriate action to take when not the formal facilitator.

References

Brassard, Michael. (1989). *The Memory Jogger Plus+®*. Methuen, MA: GOAL/QPC.

Bridges, William. (1980). *Transitions: Making Sense of Life's Changes.* Reading, MA: Addison-Wesley.

Burley-Allen, Madelyn. (1995). *Listening: The Forgotten Skill, A Self-Teaching Guide.* 2d ed. New York: John Wiley.

Geier, John G., & Downey, Dorothy E. (1989). *Energetics of Personality.* Minneapolis: Aristos Publishing House.

Katzenbach, Jon R., & Smith, Douglas K. (1993). *The Wisdom of Teams: Creating the High-Performance Organization.* Boston: Harvard Business School Press.

Keirsey, David, & Bates, Marilyn. (1984). *Please Understand Me: Character and Temperament Types.* Del Mar, CA: Prometheus Nemesis Book Company.

Kuhn, Thomas. (1962). *The Structure of Scientific Revolution.* Chicago: University of Chicago Press.

Lewin, Kurt. (1951). *Field Theory in Social Science.* New York: Harper & Row.

Merrill, David W., & Reid, Roger H. (1981). *Personal Styles and Effective Performance.* Radnor, PA: Chilton Book Company.

Nevis, Edwin C. (1987). *Organizational Consulting: A Gestalt Approach.* Cleveland: Gestalt Institute of Cleveland Press.

Schein, Edgar H. (1988). *Process Consultation, Volume I: Its Role in Organization Development.* Reading, MA: Addison-Wesley.

Kilmann, Ralph H., & Thomas, Kenneth W. (1975). Interpersonal Conflict-Handling Behavior as Reflections of Jungian Personality Dimensions. *Psychological Reports, 37,* 971–980.

Tuckman, Bruce W. (1965). Development Sequence in Small Groups. *Psychological Bulletin, 63*(6).

Weaver, Richard G. (1993). *A Dynamic Model of Systems Change: The Interaction Between Forces for Change and Forces for Stability.* Ann Arbor, MI: University Microfilms.

Instruments

DISC Instruments

Behavior Indicator©, included in: Geier, John G., & Downey, Dorothy E. (1989). *Energetics of Personality*. Minneapolis: Aristos Publishing House.

Personal Profile Analysis 3®. TIMS Management Systems, Inc. Call 1-800-528-5153 for the distributor in your area.

Personal Profile System®. Carlson Learning Company. Call 1-800-777-9897 for the distributor in your area.

Jung-based Instruments

Keirsey Temperment Sorter®, included in: Keirsey, David, & Bates, Marilyn. (1984). *Please Understand Me: Character and Temperament Types*. Del Mar, CA: Prometheus Nemesis Book Company.

Myers-Briggs Type Inventory®. Palo Alto, CA: Consulting Psychologists Press. Call 1-816-444-3500 to reach the Association of Type Psychologists for a referral to local psychologists who administer and interpret the MBTI®. Consulting Psychologists Press can be reached, for information about the instrument and the certification process, at http://www.mbti.com.

Index

Italicized page references indicate tables or figures.

About the Authors

Dr. **Richard G. Weaver** and **John D. Farrell** are internationally recognized for their expertise in helping organizations successfully implement teams, in coaching executives to lead and manage teaming environments more effectively, and in helping individuals become highly skilled facilitators. They have worked with organizations in Africa, Asia, Eastern and Western Europe, the Middle East, and North and South America. For the past two years they have been collaborating in both research and organizational consulting.

Richard G. Weaver is a consultant, facilitator, speaker, trainer, and executive coach with an extensive background in the dynamics of organizational change. Using his highly interactive style, he has created experiences through which clients have galvanized into teams, explored the barriers to their success, and identified and executed their most productive action plans. He has worked extensively with such clients as AT&T, AMOCO Production Company, and Chrysler Corporation.

Dr. Weaver has worked in social agencies (from Group and Family Worker to Executive Director) and in business (Marketing Manager at the International Small Enterprise Development Center and Director of Quality Service Management at the Carlson Companies), and for the last six years has run his own successful consulting firm, New Possibilities. Dr. Weaver has a Master of Science in Education (University of Dayton), Master of Business Administration (Wright State University), and a Ph.D. in Human and Organizational Systems (The Fielding Institute).

John D. Farrell is a consultant, facilitator, speaker, trainer, and executive coach with an extensive background in strategic planning and management. Using his business and facilitation skills he has helped a wide variety of organizations develop new strategies, achieve goals, and create more productive, supportive work environments. His clients have included AT&T, the University of Minnesota, the Greater Minneapolis Chamber of Commerce, Hennepin County, Ramsey County, the Pillsbury Company, and Mike Veeck and the Saint Paul Saints Professional Baseball Club.

After earning a Bachelor of Science degree in Chemical Engineering (University of Illinois), Mr. Farrell held management positions in the chemical industry (Technical Service Engineer with Dow Corning Corporation) and the food industry (Research Manager and Manager of Vendor Quality Improvement with The Pillsbury Company). He is currently Vice President of Member Services for the Greater Minneapolis Chamber of Commerce and founder of his own consulting firm, Facilitation Experts.

Berrett-Koehler Publishers

BERRETT-KOEHLER is an independent publisher of books, periodicals, and other publications at the leading edge of new thinking and innovative practice on work, business, management, leadership, stewardship, career development, human resources, entrepreneurship, and global sustainability.

Since the company's founding in 1992, we have been committed to supporting the movement toward a more enlightened world of work by publishing books, periodicals, and other publications that help us to integrate our values with our work and work lives, and to create more humane and effective organizations.

We have chosen to focus on the areas of work, business, and organizations, because these are central elements in many people's lives today. Furthermore, the work world is going through tumultuous changes, from the decline of job security to the rise of new structures for organizing people and work. We believe that change is needed at all levels—individual, organizational, community, and global—and our publications address each of these levels.

We seek to create new lenses for understanding organizations, to legitimize topics that people care deeply about but that current business orthodoxy censors or considers secondary to bottom-line concerns, and to uncover new meaning, means, and ends for our work and work lives.

See next page for other books from Berrett-Koehler Publishers

Other leading-edge business books
from Berrett-Koehler Publishers

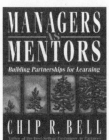

Managers As Mentors
Building Partnerships for Learning
Chip R. Bell

MANAGERS AS MENTORS is a provocative guide to helping associates grow and adapt in today's tumultuous organizations. Chip Bell's hands-on, down-to-earth advice takes the mystery out of effective mentoring, teaching leaders to be the confident coaches integral to learning organizations.

Hardcover, 200 pages, 6/96 • ISBN 1-881052-92-3 CIP
Item no. 52923-187 $24.95

Paperback, 1/98 • ISBN 1-57675-034-5 CIP • **Item no. 50345 $16.95**

Empowerment Takes More than a Minute
Ken Blanchard, John Carlos, and Alan Randolph

EMPOWERMENT TAKES MORE THAN A MINUTE is the book that finally goes beyond the empowerment rhetoric to show managers how to achieve true, lasting results in their organizations. These expert authors explain how to empower the workforce by moving from a command-and-control mindset to a supportive, responsibility-centered environment in which all employees have the opportunity and responsibility to do their best. They explain how to build ownership and trust using three essential keys to making empowerment work in large and small organizations.

Hardcover, 140 pages, 12/96 • ISBN 1-881052-83-4 CIP
Item no. 52834-187 $20.00

Paperback, 1/98 • ISBN 1-57675-033-7 CIP • **Item no. 50124 $12.00**

Getting to Resolution
Turning Conflict Into Collaboration
Stewart Levine

STEWART LEVINE gives readers an exciting new set of tools for resolving personal and business conflicts. Marriages run amuck, neighbors at odds with one another, business deals gone sour, and the pain and anger caused by corporate downsizing and layoffs are just a few of the conflicts he addresses.

Hardcover, 200 pages, 3/98 • ISBN 1-57675-005-1 CIP
Item no. 50051-264 $19.95

Available at your favorite bookstore, or call (800) 929-2929

On-The-Level
Performance Communication That Works
New Edition
Patricia McLagan and Peter Krembs

D ESIGNED TO HELP managers and employees plan and execute more effective and less fearful communication, *On The Level* provides tips, action steps, and practical tools to help everyone in and around the workplace communicate "on-the-level."

Paperback, 140 pages, 8/95 • ISBN 1-881052-76-1 CIP
Item no. 52761-264 $19.95

301 Ways to Have Fun at Work
Dave Hemsath and Leslie Yerkes
Illustrated by Dan McQuillen

I N THIS ENTERTAINING and comprehensive guide, Hemsath and Yerkes show readers how to have fun at work-everyday. Written for anyone who works in any type of organization, *301 Ways to Have Fun at Work* provides more than 300 ideas for creating a dynamic, fun-filled work environment.

Paperback, 300 pages, 6/97 • ISBN 1-57675-019-1 CIP
Item no. 50191-264 $14.95

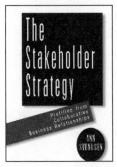

The Stakeholder Strategy
Profiting from Collaborative Business Relationships
Ann Svendsen

T HE STAKEHOLDER STRATEGY offers a step-by-step guide that companies can use to forge a network of powerful and profitable collaborative relationships with all of their stakeholders—employees, customers, suppliers, and even communities. Ann Svendsen uses easy-to-grasp concepts from everyday life, such as the process we go through in finding a mate or developing a long-term friendship, along with real-world examples to illustrate practical relationship-building strategies.

Hardcover, 252 pages 10/98 • ISBN - 1-57675-047-7 CIP
Item no. 50477-264 $27.95

Available at your favorite bookstore, or call (800) 929-2929

Put the Leading-Edge
Business Practices You Read About
to Use in Your Work and in Your Organization

D O EVER YOU WISH there was a forum in your organization for discussing the newest trends and ideas in the business world? Do you wish you could explore the leading-edge business practices you read about with others in your company? Do you wish you could set aside a few hours every month to connect with like-minded coworkers or to get to know others in your business community?

If you answered yes to any of these questions, then the answer is simple: Start a business book reading group in your organization or business community. For step-by-step advice on how to do just that, visit the Berrett-Koehler website at <www.bkpub.com> and click on "Reading Groups." There you'll find specific guidelines to help in all aspects of creating a successful reading group—from locating interested participants to selecting books, and facilitating discussions.

These guidelines were created as part of the Business Literacy 2000 program launched by the Consortium for Business Literacy—a group of 19 business book publishers whose primary goal has been to promote the formation of business reading groups within corporations and business communities. Business Literacy 2000 is dedicated to providing you with tools to help you build a dialog with others in your company or business community, share ideas, build lasting relationships, and bring new ideas and knowledge to bear in your work and organizations.

For more information on the Business Literacy 2000 program, guidelines for starting a business book reading group, or to browse or download the study guides that are available for our books, please visit our website at: <www.bkpub.com>.

If you do not have internet access, you may request information by contacting us at:

Berrett-Koehler Publishers
450 Sansome St., Suite 1200
San Francisco, CA 94111
Tel (415) 288-0260
Fax (415) 362-2512
Email bkpub@bkpub.com

Please be sure to include your name, address, telephone number, and the information you would like to receive.